MENTORING
in the
LIBRARY

ALA Guides for the Busy Librarian

Hiring, Training, and Supervising Library Shelvers
by Patricia Tunstall

Writing and Publishing: The Librarian's Handbook
edited by Carol Smallwood

MENTORING
in the
LIBRARY

BUILDING FOR THE FUTURE

MARTA K. LEE

ala AMERICAN LIBRARY ASSOCIATION
CHICAGO 2011

Marta K. Lee, BS, MA, MLS, has worked as an associate librarian at Regent University Library, in Virginia Beach, Virginia, and as an assistant librarian at Washington Theological Union, in Washington, D.C. Lee has written articles on distance learning, instruction, mentoring, interlibrary loan, public libraries, and reference services. She resides in southeastern Virginia with her husband of thirty-six years.

© 2011 by the American Library Association. Any claim of copyright is subject to applicable limitations and exceptions, such as rights of fair use and library copying pursuant to Sections 107 and 108 of the U.S. Copyright Act. No copyright is claimed in content that is in the public domain, such as works of the U.S. government.

ISBN: 978-0-8389-3593-4

Printed in the United States of America
15 14 13 12 11   5 4 3 2 1

While extensive effort has gone into ensuring the reliability of the information in this book, the publisher makes no warranty, express or implied, with respect to the material contained herein.

Library of Congress Cataloging-in-Publication Data
Lee, Marta K.
  Mentoring in the library : building for the future / Marta K. Lee.
    p. cm. -- (ALA guides for the busy librarian)
  Includes bibliographical references and index.
  ISBN 978-0-8389-3593-4 (alk. paper)
  1. Mentoring in library science--United States. I. Title.
  Z668.5.L44 2011
  020.71'55--dc22
                                                    2010003566

Book design in Charis SIL and Caecilia by Casey Bayer.

♾ This paper meets the requirements of ANSI/NISO Z39.48-1992 (Permanence of Paper).

ALA Editions also publishes its books in a variety of electronic formats. For more information, visit the ALA Store at www.alastore.ala.org and select eEditions.

ALA Editions purchases fund advocacy, awareness, and accreditation programs for library professionals worldwide.

*This book is dedicated to my husband, James Lee,
who stood by me while I wrote and edited the manuscript.
It is also dedicated to all those librarians who have seen the
benefit of mentoring and took up the call to assist others.*

CONTENTS

Appendixes

PREFACE

When I was a child, I loved using the local public library, especially during summer vacation. I visited the library twice a week, every week for the entire summer. "Books became her friends and there was one for every mood. . . . On that day when she first knew she could read, she made a vow to read one book a day as long as she lived."[1] Like Francine in *A Tree Grows in Brooklyn,* I love reading; books are my friends. In high school, I decided to pursue a library career so I might read all day like I thought librarians did. Since beginning work as a professional librarian, I have learned that librarians do not sit around all day reading like I thought they did as a child.

Over the years I found that the most important part of being a librarian is mentoring. Mentoring does not mean helping only those looking at becoming a library professional but helping anyone needing assistance. In my current academic position, as most librarians, I mentor students daily through the library. Often they are stressed over not being able to locate what they need. Just sitting next to patrons and helping them find the book or article needed enables them to replicate the same procedures to help themselves, and this makes happy students. Mentoring can be used in public, school, special, or academic libraries. It involves your knowledge. You have a commodity that others are able to tap into, gain knowledge from, and use to make a difference in the world. In addition to mentoring, sharing knowledge with others is vital. Passing on knowledge to others can make the world a better place.

A better place means taking the time to listen to individuals who need assistance. Library school students come with various needs, different needs as classes change. They might need to attend a public library board meeting, to complete an internship, or to ask a librarian questions regarding an assignment. You can be that individual who makes a difference for someone else, just like someone made a difference in your life. Over the years I have been touched by many: Judith Atwater, middle school librarian, Jeanne Klesch, Audrey Amerski, Robert Sivigny, and Jon Ritterbush, all of whom are librarians extraordinaire. Each person gave me back more than I could possibility have given him or her. Writing this book enabled me to realize how I have been helped and how I have assisted others along my life's path.

Be open to mentoring opportunities everywhere. For example, attending American Library Association (ALA) conferences provides opportunities to help others in the field. In the past I have taken advantage of résumé reviewing at the annual conference, and this involved only an hour of my time. Many of the individuals seeking assistance with their résumés were just entering the field. By taking the time to look at someone's résumé, you can find out what new librarians learned in library school.

Mentoring in the workplace requires library administration support; if you have this support, you can do wonders for others. For those longer mentoring opportunities, have a plan whenever possible. Having a plan enables the supervisor-trainee relationship to proceed smoother and provides for better evaluation upon completion. Remember, mentoring relationships benefit all involved. I hope that you gain something beneficial from this book to use in your professional career.

NOTE

1. Betty Smith, *A Tree Grows in Brooklyn* (New York: Noble and Noble), 164.

ONE

INTRODUCTION TO MENTORING

Prior to developing the idea of mentoring in the library, the term *mentor* should be defined. *The Oxford English Dictionary* defines *mentor* as a descriptive form of the proper name Mentor. Linguistically, the word can be traced back to mean advisor, from the men, to remember, think, and counsel. The Oxford dictionary further defines mentor as "an experienced and trusted counselor."[1] *Mentor,* as a term, has many synonyms that may be used interchangeably; these synonyms include *teacher, advisor,* and *guide.*[2]

Why do people need mentors? Developing and growing professionally can be difficult for the individual entering into the workforce after graduating from high school, college, or graduate school. Young people are not always aware of where to go to learn the ropes of the job or who to speak with regarding joining a professional association. Having a mentoring program available in the workplace can be helpful to those who strive to grow professionally. Implementing mentoring programs in the library can benefit all individuals involved; the supervisor can share accumulated knowledge with the trainee, the trainee learns about a new area that is being mentored, and in many cases, a relationship develops between the two colleagues.

Mentoring in the workplace is often referred to as coaching and may be defined as a "private tutor who prepares a candidate for an examination."[3]

Coaching or mentoring can be thought of as a way to provide instruction or training that allows skills to be developed. Margaret Law points out that coaching is an activity directed at building on existing skills or improving these skills, whereas mentoring is geared toward one individual assisting another to broaden the trainee's perspective.[4] For the purpose of this book, the term *mentoring* will be used to discuss how the supervisor, teacher, or manager benefits the trainee, student, or team member.

> *Implementing mentoring programs in the library can benefit all individuals involved; the supervisor can share accumulated knowledge with the trainee, the trainee learns about a new area that is being mentored, and in many cases, a relationship develops between the two colleagues.*

SOME BACKGROUND ON MENTORING

Mentoring or coaching is not a new idea. Judith Field states that mentoring occurred as early as the sixth century BC. In a 2001 article, Field references a book written by Shu Chin entitled *Chinese Book of History;* Field states that Shu Chin maintains that individuals seeking mentoring shall rule the earth.[5] In ancient China, individuals became skilled workers through apprenticeships. Apprentices would work under a master for a period of one to three years in order to learn a new trade. Once the exit tests were completed, the apprentice would then be able to conduct the work independently.[6] Library staff can benefit from a type of "apprenticeship" or mentorship in that the individual is learning from a more experienced staff member.

Mentoring relationships revolve around two individuals: a supervisor and a trainee. The supervisor acts as a guide, a coach, and a motivator but can also become a friend and confidant. The trainee may be defined as an individual who is being mentored but also may be referred to as a protégé[7] or an apprentice.[8] The term *mentee* is often used in mentoring and it alludes to a less-formal relationship, a relationship in which a friendship may grow. The supervisor needs good communication skills to make the mentoring relationship work. According to V. Heidi Hass and Tony White, good communication skills include "active listening, paraphrasing, clarifying, and feedback."[9] The supervisor should

- expect excellence;
- affirm others;

- coach, teach, and impart knowledge to others;
- be encouraging and supportive;
- promote growth and creativity; and
- provide counsel in difficult times.

These are just a few characteristics and responsibilities that make excellent leaders. Librarians use these characteristics as an ideal to strive for in mentoring, but they also attempt to remain flexible, to continue to learn, and to improve.[10]

Skills that trainees should have include the ability to communicate, organize, manage time, and maintain realistic expectations. According to Hass and White, trainees' characteristics and responsibilities include the following:

- enthusiasm;
- loyalty;
- dedication;
- a strong desire to learn;
- initiative; and
- good listening skills.[11]

Further, mentoring relationships need a welcoming environment. Ideally, both the supervisor and trainee will have good listening skills and respect for each other's opinions. The supervisor should use examples to illustrate library experiences that he or she has dealt with in the past. Limits need to be established whenever appropriate, but the supervisor should remain open to change. At the end of a mentoring period, collaboration between the supervisor and the trainee is a real possibility; for example, Doreen Harwood and Charlene McCormack presented their experiences at a 2007 conference on their collaborative project.[12] Harwood and McCormack point out that a pilot library intern program dealing with the growth of research assistance from business students was established at the University of Washington–Bothell. Interns collaborated with the faculty and the business librarian to build "Web-based tutorials for business assignments."[13] The collaboration became a way to entice business students to enter the library field.

> *Benefits for the trainees include gaining promotions, higher salaries, and career satisfaction.*

There are benefits of mentoring for the organization, for the individual acting as trainer, and for the protégé. The organization benefits from a higher level of employee retention and a more efficient introduction of newly hired employees to the company. The librarian doing the training benefits from experiencing satisfaction in helping a colleague, developing a renewed purpose in the profession, and being recognized by the organizational leadership. Benefits for the trainees include gaining promotions, higher salaries, and career satisfaction.[14]

ESTABLISHING A MENTORING PROJECT

Prior to beginning a mentoring project, the supervising librarian should spend some time communicating with the trainee via phone or e-mail to determine what the associate expects from the relationship. Do the trainee's expectations involve cataloging, experience in reference services, or assistance in developing a dossier for promotion? Whatever the situation, the mentoring should address these individual needs. In addition, the managing librarian must be committed to the idea of facilitating others in career development. Furthermore, the mentor should be self-confident and not have a personal agenda.[15]

Mentoring can be completed in an informal situation or in a formal setting. Informal programs are established when two individuals come together unofficially for one of the individuals to gain assistance. Even though many professionals willingly mentor colleagues, often they are left on their own to determine what is needed and to implement the help needed. According to Barry Sweeny, informal mentoring often can be inadequate, so formal mentoring programs are established.[16] Formal programs are set up within the organization and have prescribed requirements and procedures. This type of program is often overseen by the head of the department.

Sweeny provides factors to consider when establishing both informal and formal mentoring. Factors to consider when contemplating informal mentoring follow:

- Low expectations make mentoring easier but less effective.
- Little to no training is needed to begin the mentoring process.
- Often, employees who use or desire mentoring do not ask for assistance because they do not wish to appear "dumb."
- Often, experienced employees are reluctant to volunteer because they do not want to appear to be a know-it-all.
- Often, the workload and the need to be productive can overwhelm the desire to take the time needed to help others learn.

Consideration factors for formal mentoring follow:

- More training is required with this type of mentoring.
- Employees who desire to grow professionally or need assistance expect to ask questions.
- Veteran librarians know that collaboration is expected and desired. These individuals are able to handle the challenges of mentoring with finesse and skill.
- Knowing who is acting as mentor allows the organization, in this case the library, to provide an appropriate reward.[17]

In a 2001 article, Lois Kuyper-Rushing divides mentoring into three distinct areas: informal, supervisory, and institutional. Informal mentoring allows for a senior librarian to help a newly hired librarian become familiar with and ultimately participate in the library's culture. Supervisory mentoring involves the newly hired librarian receiving basic orientation information; this is often completed by the supervising librarian. Institutional mentoring is overseen by the personnel director as it involves documentation and explanations (e.g., tax forms or retirement benefits).[18] Supervisory and institutional mentoring are considered to be formal as they are set up to handle the daily business operations of the library.

Hass and White state that formal mentoring programs can be part of a library program or part of an association.[19] According to Sha Li Zhang, Susan J. Matveyeva, and Nancy Deyoe, "Formal mentoring programs are increasingly recognized as a means of recruitment and retention in a library setting."[20] Formal programs are established to assist librarians in gaining promotion and adapting to a new position or to an entirely new library. Library associations provide mentoring to assist librarians when they are new to the field or new to the association and desire to become involved with a committee.

The following techniques are useful when establishing a successful, effective mentoring program:

- Set goals.
- Gain an understanding of the individual situation.
- Build on self-knowledge prior to beginning the relationship.
- Deal with all roadblocks as they occur.
- Think creatively when entering the relationship.
- Build a wide network of influence, learning, and support.

In truth, "Development of successful mentoring programs is a creative process."[21] Mentoring programs take time and effort to work, and there is no guarantee that each mentoring relationship will be successful. Be prepared to spend time thinking, making decisions, having discussions, correcting errors, making changes, and experiencing successes along with failures.[22]

By playing an important role in the lives of library trainees, librarians show belief in the individuals along with providing the trainees with encouragement and affirmation. Walter C. Wright Jr. points out that "the mentoring relationship is an intentional, exclusive, intensive, voluntary relationship between two persons."[23] Providing time and building confidence are invaluable gifts for anyone. Even so, realization of the gifts they received sometimes comes too late for trainees to appropriately thank the mentors. Frequently, the trainee will provide this gift to others by becoming a mentor, thus providing the experience for someone else.

Keep in mind that even with the information provided on the attributes of good mentors, trainee characteristics, and techniques that make good mentoring programs, "Mentoring cannot be reduced to a formula."[24] Mentoring can be viewed as framework in which individuals can place their experience in a way so that others may "interact with it, make sense of it, take ownership of it, and work at reaching new levels of humanity and leadership on their own."[25] Max De Pree and Walter Wright further state that "mentoring [is] about lifelong learning."[26] Many of us learn on a daily basis without realizing that we are learning. For example, how many of us still believe as we did when we were ten or twenty? We continue to progress and learn throughout life. Working in a library makes learning somewhat different because we are constantly helping others find information; we learn from each information encounter and add it to our knowledge, which we can pass on to others by mentoring.

Mentoring in the library comes in several venues; these venues include working with a library school intern, orienting a new librarian on how a particular library operates, providing guidance to a librarian switching from technical services to reference, or advising on drafting a dossier for promotion. Mentoring discussed in this book largely stems from the perspective of the academic library but could easily be used as a model for a public, special, or school library. Each case study examines a mentoring experience with various librarians, students, or staff. In addition, library volunteers are examined in chapter 7, because volunteers mentor others while at times they are also being mentored.

NOTES

1. *The Oxford English Dictionary* 9 (Oxford: Clarendon Press, 2000), 614.
2. Judith Field, "Mentoring: A Natural Act for Information Professionals?" *New Library World* 102, no. 1166/1167 (2001): 269.
3. *The Oxford English Dictionary* 3 (Oxford: Clarendon Press, 2000), 380.
4. Margaret Law, "Mentoring Programs: In Search of the Perfect Model," *Feliciter* 3 (2001): 146.
5. Field, 270.
6. Sha Li Zhang, Susan J. Matveyeva, and Nancy Deyoe, "From Scratch: Developing an Effective Mentoring Program," *Chinese Librarianship: An International Electronic Journal* 24 (2007), www.iclc.us/cliej/cl24ZDM.html.
7. *Merriam-Webster.com,* www.merriam-webster.com/dictionary/mentee.
8. Field, 270.
9. V. Heidi Hass and Tony White, "Mentorship Task Force Report, Professional Development Committee, ARLIS/NA." *Art Documentation* 24, no. 2 (2005): 50.
10. Ibid.
11. Ibid.
12. Doreen Harwood and Charlene McCormack, "Growing Our Own: Mentoring Undergraduate Students," *Journal of Business and Finance Librarianship* 13, no. 3 (2008): 210.
13. Ibid., 201.
14. Gail Munde, "Beyond Mentoring: Toward the Rejuvenation of Academic Libraries," *Journal of Academic Librarianship* 26, no. 3 (May 2000): 172.
15. Field, 271.
16. Barry Sweeny, "Is Informal or Formal Mentoring Needed?" International Mentoring Association web page (2001), www.mentoring-association.org/Formalinformal.html.
17. Ibid.
18. Lois Kuyper-Rushing, "A Formal Mentoring Program in a University Library: Components of a Successful Experiment," *Journal of Academic Librarianship* 27, no. 6 (November 2001): 441.
19. Hass and White, 50.
20. Sha Li Zhang, Matveyeva, and Deyoe, n.p.
21. Ibid.
22. Ibid.
23. Walter C. Wright Jr., *The Gift of Mentors* (Pasadena, CA: De Pree Leadership Center, 2001), 2.
24. Max De Pree and Walter C. Wright Jr., *Mentoring: Two Voices* (Pasadena, CA: De Pree Leadership Center, 2003), 2.
25. Ibid., 2–3.
26. Ibid., 5.

TWO

MENTORING INTERNSHIPS

During job interviews, the interviewer does not always ask about the job seeker's grade-point average, but he or she does ask about library experience. It is a common occurrence of "practicing librarians [to] insist on experience when hiring newly graduated librarians."[1] Why do librarians want experience? Library schools do not teach everything individuals need to know to be a good librarian; this knowledge often comes from on-the-job experience.[2] So how can library staff expect experience when the individual is barely out of library school? Betsy McKenzie and Jim Milles state that to gain job experience, students should seek full-time library experience while working on their degree; part-time experience is also a plus. Moreover,

> *Library schools do not teach everything individuals need to know to be a good librarian.*

the individual is often provided tuition remission while working full time and taking classes part time. Another option is to find employment as a student worker in the general campus library or work as a graduate assistant in the library.[3]

During the early 1970s I took a work-study position in the Acquisitions Department at the University of Colorado Library. This position reinforced my earlier decision to become a librarian. Along the way to acquiring a library degree, I worked as a volunteer in a public library, a school library, and obtained a part-time job at a special library. This job experience helped me when I applied for my first job, and now, as a university reference librarian, I help others gain library work experience.

UNPAID AND PAID INTERNSHIPS

To help students gain work experience, library academic programs offer the opportunity of an internship or a practicum. These are very similar in their requirements, which state that the experience should be in one department, but the student should also observe what goes on in the other departments.[4] Internships and practicums allow library students the opportunity to develop their skills in the area in which they choose to work as a librarian. Internships can be paid or unpaid; often universities offer unpaid internships in exchange for three credit hours, paid through tuition dollars. An internship may be defined as an individual working in a temporary position that provides on-the-job training

The Department of Labor's Fair Labor Standards Act established six criteria that define the unpaid internship. These criteria are as follows:

1.   The training, even though it includes actual operations of the facilities of the employers, is similar to that which would be given in a vocational school.

2.   The training is for the benefit of the student.

3.   The student does not displace a regular employee, but works under the close observation of a regular employee or supervisor.

4.   The employer provides the training and derives no immediate advantage from the activities of the student; and on occasion, the operations may actually be impeded by the training.

5.   The student is not necessarily entitled to a job at the conclusion of the training period.

6.   The employer and the student understand that the student is not entitled to wages for the time spent training.

Of course, there are loopholes to each criterion. To avoid being taken advantage of, university career service advisors generally agree that all unpaid interns should have a clearly defined supervisor and structured program for the duration of the internship.[5]

Paid internships are more common in certain fields; these fields may include medicine, engineering, business, and technology. Internships with nonprofit organizations and think tanks are usually unpaid. An internship that provides a small stipend for the intern can be referred to as a partially paid internship.

DECISIONS BEFORE INTERNSHIPS

Before students explore the possibility of doing an internship, they should have completed the basic core classes and have a certain amount of knowledge regarding the area in which they select to gain work experience. For example, to do a cataloging internship, they should have completed the basic core classes in addition to having taken a cataloging course. Similarly, a reference internship means that the student has taken a reference course and understands how electronic databases work. Without the student having basic competency, the teaching librarian will have to handle a certain amount of basic instruction, which takes away from the work experience that an internship provides.

Many library school students decide early on whether to be a media specialist, an academic librarian, a special librarian, or a public librarian. Deciding on a specific type of library allows students to take the appropriate courses and to do an internship in a library that will benefit their career most. For example, a student deciding to be a media specialist would select a school library in which to do an internship. Being a media specialist can lead the librarian to feel isolated as often there is only one media specialist per school. Many do not have the opportunity to meet with other media specialists in their district.[6] So it is very important for the new media specialist to have connections. An internship offers this type of connection prior to entering the field, and many media specialists will "volunteer to be a cooperating teacher to a future library media specialist."[7] The connection can aid the new media specialist later, when he or she can ask questions of the internship supervisor via phone or e-mail. Gaining experience in the area of being a media specialist will help to develop the librarian in the skills needed for any area of specialty. Other librarians offer to be mentors to future librarians to assist them in learning more about the field, including what works and what doesn't work.

SETTING UP THE INTERNSHIP

Prior to taking on a library school intern, the hosting library and the managing librarian should have an understanding of what an internship means. The following checklist will assist in setting up the internship.

- Have a clear understanding of what [you] expect the intern to accomplish during the internship.
- Expectations should be clearly communicated to the intern from the beginning.
- Assignments should be challenging and provide the intern with a reasonable time to complete the tasks.
- Provide the intern/student with meaningful feedback throughout the internship; this is very important for the student is learning and needs positive and negative feedback.
- Be available to the student throughout the internship for questions and just plain discussion. Discussion can be vital to the intern learning. Availability can be as simple as having the intern shadow the managing librarian at the reference desk, assisting in answering queries that staff or patrons have, or inviting the intern to attend library meetings.
- Exposing the intern to various aspects of the library allows [him or her] to gain a complete picture of library operations.
- Finally, the student intern should be treated with respect.[8]

Patricia Warren states that an internship provides an opportunity to "learn from professionals, adding a dimension to their education that simply cannot be matched in the classroom."[9] Practical experience in an internship allows the student to see unique issues in a live library experience; often these experiences are not covered in the course work. She also points out that librarians and staff spend much time on technology (e.g., fixing printers or computers). According to Warren, administrators should predetermine all aspects of the internship prior to the student beginning work in the library. Interns should not be used to fill an empty slot so as to negate hiring a librarian or library assistant. The individual supervising the internship should be committed to the job and not feel pushed into the job. Finally, the intern should view the practicum or internship as a professional assignment and dress and act appropriately.[10]

Universities have different requirements for internships or practicums. The School of Library and Information Studies at the University of Alabama requires students to fill out a form in order to do an internship (see appendix

A). The program at the University of Alabama requires "one hundred fifty hours of unpaid, meaningful work to earn three hours of course credit."[11] Students are required to keep a journal of activities completed during the internship, create a log of the hours worked, and write a two- to three-page paper discussing the internship experience. The librarian hosting the intern will submit an evaluation of the work completed. The internship coordinator will provide a pass or fail grade.[12]

The Catholic University of America (CUA), in Washington, D.C., offers practicums to students of the School of Library and Information Science (SLIS). According to the SLIS web page, http://slis.cua.edu, the practicum experience

> is ultimately the only way to integrate the theories, skills and knowledge taught in the classroom with the real, daily operation of libraries. That is why the School of Library and Information Science offers students the opportunity to complete a practicum as part of their coursework. As the only library science school in Washington, D.C., SLIS is uniquely positioned to offer internship or practicum experiences in world-class institutions. Our location in the nation's capital provides opportunities that simply aren't available anywhere else.[13]

According to the course description, practicums offer the student the opportunity to gain current library experience while taking classes. Students may earn three graduate credits for working 120 hours; hours are arranged between the student and the librarian whom the student will be working with for the practicum. Practicums are graded as pass-fail and have prerequisite courses prior to the practicum. Once arrangements have been made for the practicum, the student fills out the form for enrollment in the practicum electronically (see appendix B for the CUA form). Students are required to keep a reflective journal that indicates what they completed during the practicum and to show the connections between the experience and the CUA courses taken. Upon completion of the 120 hours, the student is required to write a two-page paper describing what has been learned. The journal and paper are submitted to the practicum coordinator by the date on the syllabus.[14]

Other universities offering practicums or internships have similar guidelines and requirements. Most programs require completing a form, being in touch with the advisor, and working a set number of hours. Practicums and internships allow students to make a smooth transition from college to paid employment. In doing internships, students gain course credit, work experience, and sometimes a job offer. Internships often provide students with the only relevant work experience needed for a job;[15] this is true for many job seekers in the library field.

Internships should provide tasks that can be accomplished in the time allotted for the internship. The jobs should be professional in nature, and the supervisor should provide ample work space to complete the task, explain to the intern the rationale behind the work assigned, provide direction, and allow opportunities for feedback.[16] Internships are designed to provide students an excellent opportunity to transition from being a student to being employed. With this in mind, questions need to be asked regarding internships:

- Is or was the internship beneficial to both the student and the library?
- Was the project the intern was working on completed, or did it need to be completed?

The Syracuse University (New York) website states that the mission of the master of science in library and information science (MSLIS) is "to educate students to become leaders in the evolution of the library and information profession in the 21st century."[17] The program requires students to complete thirty-six credits to graduate and to take no more than seven years to complete the program. According to the web page, students in the library program at Syracuse University fulfill the exit requirement by completing an internship. Those students who have extensive practical experience in their chosen career area are allowed to do an independent study instead of an internship. Students are required to work 150 hours to complete the internship, and "Internships play an important role in the MSLIS program, providing opportunities to transfer concepts from the classroom into the world of information practice in libraries or other organizations."[18] Syracuse University Library School has an agreement form to be filled out as part of the planning process for the internship (see appendix C).

Case Study: A University Library Intern

In spring 2007, the dean of Regent University Library was approached by a library school student from Syracuse University who was living in the Virginia Beach area. She was interested in doing a summer internship in the reference area of an academic library. The opportunity was presented at the librarians' meeting by the library dean; several reference librarians expressed interest in working with an intern. As head of reference, I volunteered to manage the internship, to make sure that the work completed would be professional, and to answer any questions the student might have. Any questions regarding the internship may be found in an article in the winter 2009 (volume 23, number 1) issue of *Library Leadership and Management.*

As I prepared to host, supervise, and mentor the intern, I consulted the reference librarians who expressed an interest in working with an intern. Several of the librarians had special projects with which they needed assistance. These projects included assistance with the library course, in special collections, and with a political collection as well as instruction in the classroom with a liaison. Some of the projects were time sensitive and would take precedence over other projects during certain periods of the internship.

Prior to and during the internship, the instructional design (ID) librarian was working on revamping the library's online information-literacy course (Information Resources and Research—referred to as the IRR course). Just prior to the intern starting work in the library, the ID librarian provided her with access to the course as a teaching assistant. The library course is a self-paced, online course that allows students to work on the various lessons throughout the semester. Regent University Library uses *Blackboard* in making courses available for distance and local students. [19] The ID librarian asked for assistance in reviewing the course. He wanted to be sure that there was consistency and accuracy and have someone new review the course and help remove errors. After reading and completing the first six lessons, the intern took the short quiz following each lesson to make sure that the material made sense and that the questions fit the material presented. Errors or unclear materials were reported to the ID librarian to change. The librarian also wanted to know how long it took to complete each lesson in order to determine an average lesson-completion time. Knowing the estimated time to complete each lesson would allow Regent students to decide whether to do that lesson right away or return to it when they had more time to devote to it.

> *Janet Hilbun and Lynn Akin declared that for mentoring relationships to be successful the structure, objectives, assessment, and administrative and technical support should be addressed.*

The special collections librarian needed assistance reviewing older VHS and U-matic tapes to determine the contents. For preservation purposes, depending on the content, these tapes were under consideration for format change from U-matic to digital. If the tapes were relevant to a political campaign, should they be transferred to a digital format? A form was designed to provide the librarians with relevant information from each tape (see appendix D).

The intern worked with yet another librarian at Regent University Library. The librarian working as a liaison to the School of Education was approached by the school to give a presentation about the ERIC database, educator sup-port for school library media centers, and the future of libraries. The intern had worked as the media specialist for the lower grades at a private school so the liaison asked for her assistance working on this project; she felt that the intern could bring an important point of view, having worked in a school library and as a teacher. First, the intern researched databases; then, the librarian and intern collaborated on putting the presentation together. Finally, the intern attended the presentation and helped pass out materials. Being at the presentation allowed the intern to see how questions, answers, and technology problems were handled at Regent University Library's academic presentations.

Internship Prerequisites

Setting up projects was just the initial step in providing mentoring to the intern. Library literature was reviewed to see what had been written about mentoring and internships. In a 2007 article, Janet Hilbun and Lynn Akin declared that for mentoring relationships to be successful, the structure, objectives, assessment, and administrative and technical support should be addressed.[20] The library supported the internship by providing the intern with computer access (password and user name) along with space where she could complete her work. The library dean supported the internship and worked with the university food services to provide lunch each day; food services billed the library administration for the meals. The assessment and objectives were provided by the University of Syracuse, and I worked on the structure of the internship.

It is important to establish a set period of time for the internship. In this case, the hours to be worked (150) and the hours that I could give each day but still complete my regular workload were considered. The managing librarian and protégé decided that the work would be spread over six weeks at twenty-five hours per week: five hours per day, from ten in the morning until three in the afternoon, beginning in mid-June.

The schedule for the intern's day was set for a variety of work to be done each day but also for a variety of jobs to be completed. Not wanting the internship to be boring, I looked for a way to provide variety. It is important to provide the intern time at the reference desk to interact with the different librarians and to try to answer some of the questions. The special collections librarian preferred to have the intern at the same time each day so he could plan for other jobs he needed to complete. Finally, time was scheduled to handle requests from the other librarians wishing assistance with the course and classroom instruction. The following schedule was set, with the option to change the order if needed:

- 10 a.m. to noon: viewing U-matic tapes in the special collections room
- noon to 12:45 p.m.: eating lunch and discussing library issues with me
- 12:45 to 1:0 p.m.: shadowing librarians at the reference desk
- 1:30 to 3 p.m.: helping with special projects

Both the library course and classroom instruction were time sensitive, whereas other projects had lower priority, to be completed as time allowed. The U-matic tapes (part of the political collection and for special collections) were lower priority; 21 percent of the tapes in the political collection were evaluated when the internship was completed. With the shortage of staff to complete certain low-priority projects, we appreciated the intern's help. The IRR course needed to be updated prior to making it available to the students in the fall semester in early August. However, the highest priority was the classroom instruction. During the first week, the intern worked with the liaison librarian in doing a literature review and sharing her experiences working as a media specialist. The instruction to the education course took place during the morning, so the schedule was shifted that day; viewing U-matic tapes for special collections took place after lunch.

During lunch, the intern and I discussed collection development policies, scheduling issues, liaison duties, committee work, and decisions regarding adding or dropping services. At the beginning of the internship, the library was in the middle of dropping *Question Point,* a virtual reference program, and implementing instant messaging (IM). Patrons were not using the virtual reference program to ask the librarians questions. Several of the librarians felt that the program was clunky, not easy to use. When we began IM, we would receive maybe six to nine questions per week; we now receive between two to three per week. At the beginning of the fall semester, we received many queries to add us to students' buddy list. The intern and I discussed the reason for the switch: basically, the IM program was easy for the user, and patrons would not have to download anything in order to IM the library. By using *Meebo,* students are able to ask us questions from the university library web pages. During the lunchtime discussion, the intern also asked questions that came from courses she was taking through the University of Syracuse.

After lunch, the intern spent forty-five minutes at the reference desk. Shadowing librarians at the desk allowed the intern to see how different librarians handled reference questions and interacted with the patrons. In addition, she would be able to ask questions of several librarians and get a wider view of how a reference desk is handled at an academic institution. Textbooks and course work do not provide the same perspective as actual on-the-job experience.

Prior to the internship, the library dean and I discussed having the intern attend a librarians' meeting. These are not held on a regular basis during the summer because of conference attendance and vacations. One meeting was to be held during scheduled work time so she was invited to attend. Topics at the meeting included providing alumni access to select databases, changes to the IRR course, issues dealing with moving reference to a library commons, library hours, collection development, and a few updates. Attending this meeting provided the intern experience with a long agenda, a limited time frame, and how some items got postponed to the next meeting.

The American Library Association held its 2007 Annual Conference in Washington, D.C., at the end of June. Several of our librarians would be attending the meeting because of its close proximity, and several librarians are on committees. The dean decided to have many of the paraprofessionals attend for one day to visit the vendors. The library paid the staff's fees and meals and rented a large van to transport the staff to and from Washington, D.C. The dean and I discussed having the intern attend the conference for the day with the other staff members. The library paid for her fees and her meals, and she rode in the van with the staff. Upon our return from the conference, the intern and I talked about her time with the staff and visiting with the vendors. The intern emphasized that the ALA conference experience was a wonderful opportunity, although she felt the size and number of vendors was somewhat overwhelming for a first-time attendee.

> The intern "felt that the overall experience was very rewarding due to communication with the reference librarians."

The University of Syracuse sent me evaluation forms to fill out on the intern, both halfway through and at the end of the internship. The intern completed all the assigned jobs. Both projects dealing with the U-matic tapes were not expected to be finished because of the quantity of tapes needing review. In addition, both machines used to view the U-matic tapes broke multiple times. The intern performed wonderfully on reviewing the course and assisting the ID librarian with course review.

BENEFITS OF ACADEMIC LIBRARY INTERNSHIP

Mentoring provides the intern such benefits as gaining work experience and learning about what works and doesn't work with library theory. The Regent University Library internship provided structure (schedule), administrative support (the library dean), technical support (computer and access), and assessment (evaluation forms from the University of Syracuse). In the beginning of the internship, the intern and I discussed the schedule; the schedule allowed the intern to begin work without checking with me first. This was helpful in that I might be in a meeting or not at work yet when she arrived. Administrative support allowed the student to attend a librarians' meeting and to go to the ALA Annual Conference.

The intern "felt that the overall experience was very rewarding due to communication with the reference librarians."[22] Daily meetings with me provided her with insight and information about reference services. Discussing library "issues from [her] classes to see if these issues were important to the Regent University Library setting" were important to the intern.[23] The intern felt that the reference librarians totally supported the internship, and viewing answers to reference queries was beneficial. Having a somewhat varied experience helped to make the internship a true librarian experience. As all librarians know, there is not a day that is the same; we all have to jump in and handle meetings, answer questions, provide instruction, and make decisions on materials.

At the conclusion of the internship, all the librarians who worked with her stated they were impressed with the job she did for Regent University Library. The library dean, the head of access services, and I discussed hiring a half-time staff person with no benefits to work at the reference desk. I mentioned the good experience we had with the intern and stated that she would work well in that position, plus there would be no learning curve. The intern was hired to work the reference desk for twenty hours per week, four hours per day, from Monday through Friday. She would open the reference desk at eight every morning, answer e-mail messages that came in overnight, and retrieve phone messages. From eight to nine she worked the desk alone and was responsible for both IM and in-person questions; at nine a librarian arrived at the desk to work with her until noon. Starting with the spring semester of 2007, the librarian would not come out to the desk until ten. Having extra office time allowed the librarian to write or to complete or work on different projects.

Mentoring a student doing an internship was very rewarding for me as a librarian. It enabled me to realize what I had learned and to pass knowledge on to someone else. It also encouraged me to tackle additional mentoring with staff and others entering the library profession. This experience provided an opportunity to know what worked well and what didn't (for example, the U-matic players were old and broke easily, causing fewer tapes to be viewed). It is very important to establish structure, to provide feedback, and to have assessment, technical, and administrative support. The most important thing that I gained from the experience is a lifelong friend. Mentoring is very rewarding, and it won't be the last time that I do it.

NOTES

1. Betsy McKenzie and Jim Milles, "Why Do Librarians Eat Their Young? And How Law Librarians Can Make Things Better," *One Person Library* 25, no. 5 (September 2008): 7.
2. Marta Lee, "Growing Librarians: Mentorship in an Academic Library," *Library Leadership and Management* 23, no. 1 (Winter 2009): 31.
3. McKenzie and Milles, 7.
4. Ibid., 8.
5. UNIVERSUMUSA, WetFeet, www.wetfeet.com/Undergrad/Internships/Articles/Unpaid-Internships, accessed July 13, 2009.
6. Christine Meloni, "Mentoring the Next Generation of Library Media Specialists," *Library Media Connection* (January 2008): 32.
7. Ibid.
8. Patricia Warren, "Inside Internship: A Student's Perspective," *College and Undergraduate Libraries* 4, no. 1 (1997): 118.
9. Ibid., 118–23.
10. School of Library and Information Studies at the University of Alabama, www.slis.ua.edu/drupal5/.
11. Ibid.
12. Practicum with the School of Library and Information Science at Catholic University of America, http://slis.cua.edu/courses/practicum/index.cfm.
13. Catholic University of America web page, http://slis.cua.edu.
14. Marian Rothman, "Lessons Learned: Advice to Employers from Interns," *Journal of Education for Business* (January/February 2007): 140.
15. Ibid., 141.
16. Syracuse University Library School web page, http://ischool.syr.edu/academics/graduate/mls/.
17. Ibid.
18. Ibid.
19. Lee, 32.
20. Janet Hilbun and Lynn Akin, "E-mentoring for Librarians and Libraries," *Texas Library Journal* 83, no. 1 (Spring 2007): 28.

21. Cary Reynolds, intern from Syracuse University, e-mail message to the author, December 2, 2007.
22. Ibid.

THREE

MENTORING AND LIBRARY SCHOOL ASSIGNMENTS

Mentoring may involve working with an intern, as discussed in chapter 2. But library professionals can also serve as mentors to library and information services students working on class assignments. Some professors entrust their students with assignments designed to be completed by interacting with professional library staff. These assignments can range from attending a board meeting at a public library to shadowing a librarian at the reference desk.

SPECIAL LIBRARY ASSIGNMENTS

The Catholic University of America (CUA) School of Library and Information Science, located in Washington, D.C., offers a course entitled the Special Library/Information Center, which includes a site-visit project. According to the course syllabus, "Each student will choose a local special library to visit and to conduct an interview with someone who is knowledgeable about the entire library's operation."[1] Furthermore, to make the project more valuable for students, "The library should not be one where you have worked in the past or now work in, or where you have a personal relationship."[2]

As stated in the syllabus, the report is to be between ten and twelve double-spaced pages, and the details regarding format would be provided in class.

> Research should encompass such topics as fee-based services, marketing/public relations, reference, library web sites, intranets, blogs, wikis, content management systems, cataloging, training (for library staff and others), approximate budget and institutional culture. Have they moved recently, or are they planning a move? How do they add value to their organization? Does the library have a mission statement?[3]

The professor, Bruce Rosenstein, makes the point that not every library can or will be involved in each of these activities. However, the student should determine which of these activities are relevant for that particular library. Students are to give brief presentations of their findings during a class period toward the last portion of the semester. Handouts may be utilized but no technology aids, like PowerPoint, may be used for the presentation. This presentation will not be graded but is mandatory.[4] Most students are not happy about presenting in front of a class. However, it provides a running start on being in front of a group of people when the student becomes a professional librarian.

Each student will choose a local special library to visit and to conduct an interview with someone who is knowledgeable about the entire library's operation.

While working on my master's in library and information science degree at CUA during the late 1990s, I took the Special Library/Information Center course and had this same assignment. Living 150 miles south of the campus in Washington, D.C., I approached the instructor about whether a special library in my area could be visited. Upon approval, I visited the library at the Virginia Institute of Marine Science (VIMS); VIMS is located at Gloucester Point, Virginia, and is part of the College of William and Mary. The VIMS library is geared toward assisting students working on graduate degrees in the area of oceanography. I directed my questions to the library's director and used the library catalog and collection to gain additional information. Like most librarians, the director of VIMS was very gracious in helping me complete the assignment.

GENERAL COURSE ASSIGNMENTS

Another CUA library school course assignment led me to the local public library. Students were asked to attend a public library's board meeting with the library director. After the board meeting, each student would give an oral report in class on what generally took place at the board meeting, the type of items discussed, and what was voted on or resolved. Becoming acquainted with the local public library director benefits the student, as the director can be a great source of information, can provide assistance, and can be a trainer for the library school student during and after completing his or her degree. Getting to know the local public librarian enabled me to have a local mentor in the library field. She provided me with information regarding the financial side of public libraries and services they provide. We became better acquainted, and the librarian became an active part of my reference list

> *Be gracious to the librarian; obtain the information needed as quickly as possible.*

for many years. I also volunteered at the library to add to my library experience. Be courteous; you never know where your next supervisor might come from or who, in the future, might be your trainee. Try to remember someone who gave a listening ear to you and maybe offered some advice regarding course work or guidance in making a decision.

Attending board meetings or completing assignments allows students to see what the librarian does during the work day, week, or year. Plus, it provides students with professional contacts and access to different kinds of libraries and to a wider range of professionals. Remember, when visiting a library, respect the amount of time that is being taken from a busy librarian's schedule. Be gracious to the librarian; obtain the information needed as quickly as possible. As a student I decided that when I became a librarian, I would help students complete their assignments. Now that I am a practicing librarian, I have been receptive to aiding students and providing assistance whenever possible. I try to plan for the student even if he or she shadows me for only a few hours or just asks a few questions. Doing this little bit doesn't take an enormous amount of time but is extremely helpful to the student.

ASSISTING STUDENTS IN THEIR EDUCATION

Hosting students who are completing assignments is a form of mentoring. The students will "gain insight and assistance from their mentors."[5] As committed professional librarians, we should look "for mentoring opportunities in every professional activity that we become involved in."[6] Contact with students provides the perfect opportunity to assist them in entering the profession and to provide some guidance. Take the time to answer their content-related questions about the profession. Encourage them to participate in professional organizations. Promote the idea of attending professional meetings and conferences on all levels: local, state, and national. In short, help them to get involved, to expand their horizons, and to interact with other professionals who may turn out to be potential mentors as well.[7] Guidance and time are two of the most important things that you, as a professional, can provide students. You are assisting them in learning about the profession and helping them "learn about the political dynamics of the profession."[8]

> *One of the most critical issues facing the [library] profession today is finding academic librarians to replace a rapidly graying workforce.*

According to Joseph Fennewald and John Stachacz, "One of the most critical issues facing the [library] profession today is finding academic librarians to replace a rapidly graying workforce."[9] This is a good reason for those of us in the field to pass on our experience and knowledge by teaching or providing guidance to the younger librarians. How are new librarians to gain insight or experience if we, the experienced workforce, do not provide them the opportunities to grow and develop? Fennewald and Stachacz note that library schools do provide students with "opportunities to enhance their classroom experience" by assigning them to visit libraries, ask questions, and do additional research.[10] Other opportunities might include those students interested in cataloging locating a cataloger who is willing to act as a mentor, a reference course assigning students to locate a reference librarian to shadow for one hour or more, and management classes having students locate library administrators to act as mentors.[11] Such library assignments are a good way to foster ideas on what works or what does not work in the library and to discuss relevant topics with experienced librarians. A few years ago, one of the reference librarians at Regent University taught the reference course for CUA off-campus, at Norfolk. She included an assignment to locate certain reference titles. Many of the students worked together in this "scavenger hunt" of titles. It made the project go faster, and provided the students a chance to work together and collaborate.

> *How are new librarians to gain insight or experience if we, the experienced workforce, do not provide them the opportunities to grow and develop?*

Case Study: Library Degrees in Virginia

Over the years Regent University Library has been approached by library school students desiring to do an internship; we had two in 2007 alone. The library has also been approached by about a half-dozen students in recent years needing to complete class assignments. Considering that Virginia does not have a library school makes the number amazing, and we are not the only library in the state that has been approached. Students in Virginia either obtain their library degree through an online program or move to another state that offers an ALA-accredited degree. Some students have opted to pursue the media specialist endorsement taught through the teachers program at Old Dominion University. This is not an ALA-accredited program so is not what many are looking for in a library program. The Catholic University of America (CUA), in Washington, D.C., offers courses at several off-campus sites to make it easier for Virginia students to obtain their library degrees. Many students are pursuing degrees through one of the many other ALA-accredited programs that are offered online. Online classes make it especially beneficial to have assignments that put students in touch with practicing librarians.

While pursuing my library degree, I worked part–time as a library assistant in a special library. This job provided me with needed library experience and helped develop some of my management views toward workers and assisting others along the way. The library director was welcoming, but he was too busy researching, assisting in developing museum displays, and writing to provide guidance to library students. However, one of the catalogers who worked on converting the card catalog to an automated system was a wonderful mentor. She provided guidance to me on which library courses would be helpful and became a reference for me in job applications.

An online library student living in Virginia Beach asked the library dean if she could complete a library school course assignment—shadowing a librarian at the reference desk—in Regent University Library. With the dean's approval, I contacted the student and discovered she needed to spend two to three hours with a librarian at the reference desk to see how questions were handled. I had her come to the library on an afternoon when I shared the shift with another librarian. I had been assisting the librarian for several weeks because the shift was extremely busy and none of the reference desk student assistants worked during this time period.

The student gained the benefit of shadowing two librarians handling multiple queries in person, by telephone, and through instant messaging (IM) and e-mail. Many of the questions asked at the desk involved what we call an "extended reference answer" at Regent University Library; extended reference means consulting multiple sources and taking more than ten minutes to answer. Many of the reference interviews, on this day, took some time to narrow down from a vague question to one that reflected what the student really needed and desired. The catalog and several databases were consulted to locate relevant data. Some of the material needed was not available in full text in our subscription databases or the journal was not in our collection so we discussed interlibrary loan and referrals to one of the consortium-area libraries with the student.

> *"Students enrolled in online programs have found it helpful to discuss library assignments with [a] mentor."*

During the two and a half hours, the student benefited from the librarians' interactions. While answering e-mail questions, we consulted with the student on how she might answer the question and discussed how we would answer the question; often what the student suggested would be included in the answer. Between patron questions, we discussed questions from the library school student regarding library issues that came up in her classes. The student declared the experience invaluable as it showed that theory is different from actually being in the field. In theory the reference interview is similar to what is taught in the classroom, but it differs in the field as patrons are human beings who phrase questions for which no book can prepare you. Besides, patron understanding of the same assignment varies so each patron's information search will vary.

ONLINE AND DISTANCE PROGRAM MENTORING

Fennewald and Stachacz state that "students enrolled in online programs have found it helpful to discuss library assignments with [a] mentor."[12] This mentor could be any librarian who is helping them learn and providing valuable experience. In the field, librarians have an invaluable knowledge of what goes on in the library so they can provide answers that often differ from what a textbook might state. Fennewald and Stachacz point out that those students with limited library experience feel differently about advice and feedback received from their mentor than a protégé with lots of library experience. Students feel that the advice and feedback differed from the classroom theorizing. According to Fennewald and Stachacz, a student also felt that having a professional librarian who is acting, even for a short period, as a mentor is vital for those students "taking courses through distance education and [who quite possibly] may feel isolated."[13]

The most important part of assisting distance students with assignments is that the librarian should view each encounter as a chance to help a future colleague. Treat the experience as your opportunity to mentor students with their future careers. Ask the students pertinent questions regarding the projects they are working on or the types of internship they wish to undertake; listen to them and hear what they are saying. Get to know the students by asking which area of the library they are most interested in and what they expect from the library profession. In setting up the internship or the one-time visit to the library, be sure to place them in the correct location to provide the maximum benefit.[14]

Having a library student complete an assignment within the library helps to keep the librarians fresh and on the cutting edge of what library students are learning and expecting from the library profession. More important, it helps to keep the librarian abreast of what is being taught in library schools today. Since I graduated from library school, about ten years ago, a portion of the curriculum is different; this is based in part on technology changes. I took a course on online searching where the instructor used *Dialog;* courses today are broader and include more information. The course that I took is not offered anymore; other courses have replaced it. For example, CUA course LSC 610, Internet Searches and Web Design: Tools and Technologies,

> is designed for students interested in becoming skilled searchers of Internet resources and creative designers of Web sites. It will cover Internet search tools, search engine architecture, search techniques and strategies, evaluation of information resources and applications of information architecture to web site design. Through exercises, discussions, lectures, projects and presentations students will learn the strengths and limitations of search tools and the principles of user-centered Web design. In addition, students will have hands-on practice with web site creation with HTML and Dynamic HTML. They will use HTML editors such as Netscape Composer and Dreamweaver and graphic tools such as GIF Construction Kit and Fireworks to create sites with interactivity. They will also learn the basics of placing databases on the Web.[15]

This core course "introduces students to the evolving role of information systems in the storage and retrieval of information."[16] In addition, students will "explore how information technology in libraries, archives and information centers, and on the World Wide Web facilitates interaction with information."[17] During the class the students learn about several topics:

- applicable theory, standards, and principles
- the capabilities and functions of various information systems, including integrated library systems and databases
- practical technology skills used by librarians, such as working with databases and creating web pages[18]

CUA also provides courses on information services to various subjects:

- LSC 704: Humanities Information
- LSC 706: Social Science Information
- LSC 708: Science and Technology Information
- LSC 715: Organization of Internet Resources[19]

Similar to CUA, the University of Syracuse offers core courses in introductory areas and in information resources. Students take elective courses from three areas of focus:

- information services and resources
- information organization, retrieval, and access
- information systems design and management[20]

Many of the courses offered at other universities, like those at CUA, reflect the changing needs of technology. For example, courses offered at the University of Syracuse include Records Management in the Digital Age and Database Management.[21]

TIPS ON MENTORING AND LIBRARY SCHOOL ASSIGNMENTS

Helping library students complete course assignments does not consume a large amount of time, and it requires just the willingness to help. Mentors gain more than they provide; passing on advice and information to the next generation of librarians is rewarding.[22] Try to remember when you were a library school student who felt overwhelmed, had fears, and worried about choosing the correct field. Well, students today often experience the same fears. When I was a library student, I knew that I wanted to be a cataloger, *nothing* but a cataloger. My first job, as a cataloger, was interesting but stressful because students are not taught all they need to know to be a cataloger; much of cataloging is learned on the job. Newly hired cataloging librarians need to have a patient librarian who is willing to teach the ins and outs of the job. After three months of a six-month experience in cataloging, I started on my road to finding a reference position and have never looked back. A good mentor could probably have told me that cataloging was not the path for me; if I had been told by a mentor that it seemed that I liked helping people and that I might consider reference, this quite possibly could have made the difference for me to not pursue cataloging. Certainly, the cataloging experience was not all bad, and it has enabled me to be a better reference librarian. I have a better understanding of MARC records and the Library of Congress subject headings, which has aided me in my reference position.

> *Try to remember when you were a library school student who felt overwhelmed, had fears, and worried about choosing the correct field.*

Even conversations with library school students or newly graduated librarians help these individuals to gain a broader "perspective of the library profession."[23] Margaret Law states that "mentoring can provide a useful way to broaden an individual's understanding of the larger and more abstract issues of the library community."[24] Obtaining "recognition as a peer by other faculty members is a boon to . . . the library faculty."[25] Building a long-term relationship with a future librarian can be a great reward. However, this isn't always enough to entice many excellent librarians into becoming trainers or into building a mentoring program. The normal array of protests comes from librarians claiming workload prevents them from working with an intern or a student even for a few hours.

To encourage mentoring, some libraries provide an "allocation of travel money awarded to each mentor."[26] The money is used to provide assistance for professional development of the training librarian; it can also be "used to help sponsor a student's research presentation at a professional conference."[27] Providing students the opportunity to attend professional conferences helps them to grow academically and to develop into excellent colleagues. Little things you do to help someone today can mean that you are developing a mentor of the future who might help someone else along the way.

Think back to the days when you were studying to become a librarian or at your first job. Did someone act as a good mentor for you? Did this person give "you the inspiration to be a librarian"?[28] Consider what your actions say to the librarians of the future. The librarian who steps up and provides a mentoring opportunity is saying that future librarians are important and that he or she, as a current librarian, is willing to help them learn. Whereas saying that you are too busy loudly states that mentoring and helping others is unimportant. Acting as a mentor, even for an hour, can influence an individual and his or her career choice. Mentoring can point individuals in completely new directions and might just make them consider becoming mentors in the future.

NOTES

1. E-mail correspondence with Bruce Rosenstein from March 25, 2009; Rosenstein provided the information from his syllabus from LSC 818 course.
2. Ibid.
3. Ibid.
4. Ibid.
5. Joan Kaplowitz, "Mentoring Library School Students—a Survey of Participants in the UCLA/GSLIS Mentor Program," *Special Libraries* 83, no. 4 (Fall 1992): online n.p.
6. Ibid.
7. Ibid.
8. Ibid.
9. Joseph Fennewald and John Stachacz, "Recruiting Students to Careers in Academic Libraries," *College and Research Libraries News* 66, no. 2 (2005): 120.
10. Ibid.
11. Ibid.
12. Fennewald and Stachacz, 121.
13. Ibid.
14. Ibid.
15. CUA web site, http://slis.cua.edu/courses/courses.cfm.
16. Ibid.
17. Ibid.
18. Ibid.
19. Ibid.
20. University of Syracuse Library School web site, http://ischool.syr.edu/.
21. Ibid.
22. Fennewald and Stachacz, 122.
23. Margaret Law. "Mentoring Programs: In Search of the Perfect Model," *Feliciter* 3 (2001): 146.
24. Ibid., 148.
25. Cheryl Riley and Barbara Wales, "Academic Librarians and Mentoring Teams: Building Tomorrow's Doctorates." *Technical Services Quarterly* 14, no. 3 (1997): 9.

26. Ibid.

27. Ibid.

28. Andrea Sevetson, "Editor's Corner: Thanking Our Mentors," *DttP: Document to the People* 35, no. 1 (Spring 2007): 4.

FOUR

MENTORING THE
POTENTIAL LIBRARIAN

Developing an individual's interest in pursuing any career may not be easy. Often the idea has to be planted and developed over a period of weeks or years. All professional staff should actively listen to what an individual says and does. Individuals can become disillusioned about the career path they have chosen and are receptive to career suggestions. Librarian and author Antonia Olivas felt disappointed, lost, and trapped in a career field that was no longer appealing: "By the end of my senior year in college and after many semesters of student-teaching hours, I decided that teaching high school was definitely not for me."[1] Librarians at Olivas's local library, where she worked part-time while attaining her bachelor's degree, encouraged her to start a master's in library science.[2] For the individual who is receptive to different ideas, just planting the seed will allow the idea to germinate and to grow, and at this point in time, Olivas was open to thinking about such suggestions. The librarians were very supportive, pointing Olivas to scholarships and providing recommendations.[3] Like Olivas, all that some individuals may need is to have someone listen and suggest librarianship as a possible career choice.

> *By the end of my senior year in college and after many semesters of student-teaching hours, I decided that teaching high school was definitely not for me.*

MENTORING AND CAREER CHOICES

Mentoring can change and develop as the mentor acquires individual skills after mentoring a variety of individuals. Every mentoring situation is totally different; it can expand the mentor's horizon and make the mentor grow. Helping someone decide on a career choice is different from working extensively with an intern or aiding another student in passing a course. When I took courses at a community college in Michigan, the campus geography professor approached me to help another student study, as this student was failing the geography course. For the remaining portion of the semester, the student and I studied together in the campus learning center. The following semester, this student thanked me for the help and told me that she had obtained a solid B in the course. She stated that the study skills I provided helped her in her current classes, and she was appreciative regarding my assistance. This was the beginning of my mentoring others along their way toward obtaining a college degree. Following this first semester, the professor arranged for me to become a paid tutor at the community college learning center for all of his geography courses.

> Students were encouraged to attend the tutoring sessions by being offered two extra-credit points per tutoring session attended, up to twenty extra-credit points.

Students were encouraged to attend the tutoring sessions by being offered two extra-credit points per tutoring session attended, up to twenty extra-credit points. Students liked this extra-credit idea because it could mean a letter grade difference in their final grade. However, after realizing that their test grades went up after tutoring, they continued to attend tutoring sessions even after the extra credit stopped. The tutoring was handled as a discussion of the material that was presented in the lectures and from the book. The students liked the discussions as opposed to a lecture format and felt that they could ask questions in order to understand the material better. Students stated that it helped reinforce what was taught in the classroom. Many of the attending students encouraged other students to come to the tutoring sessions. Within nine months, because the number of students increased with each semester, and we needed a larger space with more tables where we could make use of maps and so forth, the learning center provided me with my own room for these tutoring sessions.

During this time, the geography professor and I became fast friends. He encouraged me in the field of geography as he perceived that I had a gift for the subject. Because of my husband's military transfer, I located a university that offered geography in southeastern Virginia. At the university I chose to attend, a geography professor became my mentor; he provided help with course selections that would help me finish the four-year degree. Part of the mentoring involved whether I ever considered going to graduate school to obtain a master's degree in library science. I had thought about it but was not sure if I could complete the necessary degrees. Because I was within a few months of finishing a bachelor's degree, doing a master's degree was not as overwhelming as it once had been. During the next three and a half years, I pursued a master's in library science from Catholic University of America (CUA) while earning a master's in humanities from the school where I obtained my undergraduate degree. I knew that my final wish was to work in an academic library so a subject master's would only be an asset in pursuing this goal. Having a second master's is not mandatory to be hired as an academic librarian, but having one is helpful.

> *Having two wonderful mentors over a period of seven years meant that I would, at any opportunity, mentor others in their academic quests.*

Having two wonderful mentors over a period of seven years meant that I would, at any opportunity, mentor others in their academic quests. Becoming a librarian has provided me with opportunities to mentor many students working on a bachelor's degree, a master's degree, or a doctorate. In addition, the academic library has given me the opportunity to provide mentoring for library school students. This includes providing potential librarians time to shadow me or other reference librarians, answering questions, and offering networking opportunities whenever possible.

Mentoring opportunities for library students have grown as more library programs gravitate to being partially or fully online. Some of the programs are a hybrid type of program, with a combination of both online and in-person classes. During the time I attended CUA, nine of the required twelve classes could be taken at one of their off-campus sites in Virginia; the remaining three courses were required to be taken on campus. The latter has since been dropped, and all courses may be taken off campus or online. Many of the courses have become available both in person and online. It is reassuring to have the flexibility to take courses on campus, off campus, or online. Many students choose to take classes all three ways. However, with online courses, it is important for students to have actual library experience and to have a librarian with whom they can ask questions. Without either, how can the student really know that the library field is the correct career choice?

Other library schools offer their library programs online because many "adults with a full-time job and home responsibilities" have trouble finding the time to attend classes.[4] Online courses allow students to complete the course work when the individual has time, which is often in the late evening when other responsibilities are finished. This flexibility is attractive to many teachers desiring to become media specialists. Time constraints and desire can be magnified when the college or university that mainly serves a rural community is a distance away. Eastern Carolina University is one such college that serves rural eastern North Carolina. Many of the students have a commute time of one to three hours one way to attend courses in the library program. Having it online has meant a savings of two to six hours drive time every day these students attend classes. Online programs are flexible, with students doing the course work when it is convenient, but many students miss the interaction of the classroom environment. Enrollment in the library program at Eastern Carolina University has increased since going online.[5] Having online college programs provide the opportunity for course assignments for the students to locate a local librarian to act as a mentor. In addition, requirements such as doing an internship or having the student interview a librarian about his or her job allow students the chance to gain insight to the library field in general and not just theory.

> *They found me on the floor with a facilities services staff member deciding how and where a hole could be drilled in the desk for computer cables.*

Over the past two years, two potential library school students have approached Regent University Library desiring to spend quality time within the library. They were wondering if becoming a librarian would be the correct occupation. The first student interested in librarianship was a daughter of a Regent University government professor; the professor brought her to the library to talk with me. The student had just finished her undergraduate degree and was deciding whether she would go to library school or pursue something in the medical field. At this time, I was working with a library intern, and the library's reference and circulation areas were in the process of moving to a combined information commons. I agreed to talk to the potential library school student. I began having her shadow me and other librarians to help her make the decision. On the days that the potential library school student would come to the library, I would first get the intern started on one of the assigned projects, then have the other student come in to discuss librarianship, to shadow library personnel, and to talk with me and other librarians regarding whether the librarian field was for her.

As head of reference, I could get called away at any time by facility services regarding the location of the reference desk, where we wanted the phones or computers located, how to change the desk to accommodate power or phone cords, or any other number of details to make the move to a commons successful. During such times, I attempted to have the potential student talk with another librarian, but when this was not possible, I would have her come with me to problem solve. I felt that this would help her see that librarianship is not always the same job, and there are many multitasking opportunities; often there are so many opportunities to multitask that it is hard to complete any job. Musician John Lennon observed that life is what happens when you are busy making other plans; well, some days multitasking is what happens when you had other plans.

One day I had the potential library school student working with the instructional design librarian when I got called away by facilities services. When the potential student was finished with the job, she and the librarian came looking for me; they found me on the floor with a facilities services staff member deciding how and where a hole could be drilled in the desk for computer cables. Seeing librarians when they are at their busiest and being pulled in multiple directions can be a benefit for those choosing whether to come into the profession. It helps the student have a more accurate picture of what the librarian does on a day-to-day basis.

The discussions with the potential library school student included the type of classes she should take to be an academic librarian, what kind of things librarians did as part of their job, why and how to take part in professional librarian associations, and many other topics. We discussed the possibility of her combining her interests and becoming a medical librarian. This student decided not to become a librarian but to go into the health field instead because she wanted to work more directly with patients.

Regent University Library had a second potential MLS school student seeking help with her career decision; she became a library volunteer as well (see chapter 7).

CHOOSING THE RIGHT AREA IN LIBRARIANSHIP

Providing potential library school students with learning opportunities can only furnish students with the right kind of experience when they become a professional. It is important to know how circulation operates, how materials are processed, how a collection is shifted, or any of the multitude of library jobs. In addition, it helps them think about the area in which they would like to work upon completing their degree.

With the current and continuing advancements in technology, library education is constantly changing and adapting. However, as Mary Ellen Bates states, library school students still need to know some basic principles:

- "Libraries are a business and you are the president of your company.
- Whatever the question, you can either find the information or find someone who can find it.
- Being a librarian means thinking creatively about information."[6]

Learning these principles does not always happen in library school; practical, on-the-job experience goes a long way in building these skills. Also having a good mentor who can assist in setting an example helps in building these skills. Even with a good mentor, there are some librarians who never learn these principles. By realizing that you are a form of a blank slate and absorbing all you can during library school, an internship, or any library opportunity, you will become a better librarian. Even after becoming a professional librarian, continue to absorb and learn as much as possible. Having graduated ten years ago, I find myself still learning from my coworkers, and definitely from the students.

Mentoring others along their way through life will only make you a better librarian. Good mentoring means providing guidance so the student can make an informed decision regarding his or her career path. Just keep in mind it is not your career path; it is their career path. Mentoring students interested in becoming librarians helps you to remember the reason you chose the profession in the first place. I try never to forget the idealism that I felt while attending library school and after I received my degree. This idealism has provided me with the ability to remember that I was a new student once—and a technology challenged one—and to be patient.

NOTES

1. Antonia Olivas, "Mentoring New Librarians: The Good, the Bad and the Ugly," in *Staff Development Strategies That Work!* by Georgie L. Donovan and Miguel A. Figueroa (New York: Neal-Schuman, 2009), 62.
2. Ibid.
3. Ibid.
4. Constance A. Mellon and Diane D. Kester, "Online Library Education Programs: Implications for Rural Students," *Journal of Education for Library and Information Science* 45, no. 3 (Summer 2004): 210.

5. Ibid., 212.

6. Mary Ellen Bates, "The Newly Minted MLS: What Do We Need to Know Today?" *Searcher* 6, no. 5 (May 1998): 30.

FIVE

DEVELOPING THE NEW
LIBRARIAN IN THE WORKPLACE

Mentoring should take place across the workplace: assisting the newly hired, orienting the brand new MLS, building a coworker's dossier for promotion, or helping colleagues wishing to become published. Mentoring in the workplace has many benefits for both the supervisor and the trainee. Benefits for the trainee include "higher salaries, promotions [and] overall career satisfaction."[1] Supervisors often find "a renewal of professional purpose . . . a sense of satisfaction that one has helped to influence the future of the profession [and the] ability to identify and advise"[2] This chapter will look at how mentoring helps a new librarian become acquainted with the job, gain assistance and experience in liaison work, and become familiar with reference services.

MENTORING THE NEWLY HIRED

Many librarians are hired to fill an entry-level position and learn while on the job.[3] Thus, many libraries provide the newly hired librarian with an orientation and often a period of mentoring during the beginning portion of the job. Many libraries provide new employees a form of orientation, which can entail spending time with the human resources department reviewing information regarding health insurance, retirement funds, and other information. In addition, newly hired librarians are given a tour of the library and campus. The newly hired librarian is often paired with a seasoned librarian to assist in learning the job and to aid in the "ongoing professional and career development for achieving [a librarian's] personal and professional goals."[4] The mentoring librarian assists the protégée in "meet[ing] the challenge of the day-to-day responsibilities."[5] Further, the mentor assists with setting long-term goals, becoming a member of a professional organization, building leadership skills, publishing, and presenting at conferences.[6]

> *Benefits for the trainee include "higher salaries, promotions [and] overall career satisfaction."*

THE DEPARTMENT HEAD AS MENTOR

The department head should be aware of talking and learning opportunities for the new librarian. Conversations with a newly hired employee enable the department head to acknowledge and remedy problems that the new hire might be having. Additionally, talking with a new hire offers the opportunity for a new staff member to gain needed training. The department head should involve the new librarian in projects that will develop the librarian professionally.[7] Department heads play an important "role in influencing the self-confidence" of all who come to work under them.[8] The department head should be aware that both positive reinforcement and constructive criticism are needed. That is, department heads can congratulate on a job well done but also point out ways to do something better. Too much criticism can discourage workers and sometimes stop them from putting in their best efforts, and it can even result in a higher rate of turnover. Although constructive criticism has its place and can be helpful, it is preferable to tone down the negative and begin by stating what the new hires are doing well.

Regent University Library has an orientation program for the newly hired and selects a mentor for the staff member's adjustment period. Adjustment periods involve time for the new hire to become oriented to the new surroundings such as where things are located and how things are done. The new hire is paired with the head of reference, because "the department head is responsible for the knowledge, skills, attitudes and values of the reference librarians."[9] The department head also needs to make sure that the librarians keep up with new technology and new developments in the library field.[10] Prior to the new librarian beginning work, the department head establishes a schedule for the new librarian's training period. However, schedules must be flexible because things happen and staff schedules often change, which means the training schedule needs to be shifted. Often, shifting the training schedule means changing multiple staff members' schedules. "The supervisor should make every effort to greet the new employee on his [her] first day."[11]

Nine and a half years ago I began working in Regent University as a reference librarian and went through an orientation period of about two months. Being a relatively new librarian, I felt that I was behind the eight ball in answering many of the questions asked at the reference desk. Even though I had good reference-interview skills, I still had much to learn in questioning, listening, and retrieving needed information. In addition, I had to learn where information was located or might be located. Skilled librarians provided mentoring in locating needed information for faculty and students. The librarian who was the most helpful was the liaison to the School of Divinity. He had a master's in divinity and had been a librarian at Regent University for eighteen years by the time I began working there. His knowledge gave me a broad base from which to locate needed information. I have attempted to absorb all that I can in order to serve the student population. In turn, this helps in mentoring the library school student, a potential library school student, or the new librarian at your library.

Sandra J. Weingart, Carol A. Kochan, and Anne Hedrich maintain that the new employee should have a checklist of what is expected during the first days on the job. The employee should also have a time frame for completing the tasks. Time is also needed for the newly hired to assimilate new information, reflect on the job, and ask questions.[12]

Case Study One: A University Library New Hire

During the summer of 2006, Regent University Library hired a librarian with systems experience to fill a reference position. The new librarian was hired to handle "digital services, be the liaison to the School of Communications and the Arts, to work as part of the reference team," and, of course, various assignments.[13] A two-week intensive schedule was established prior to the new librarian's arrival, in mid-August 2006. As noted by Weingart, Kochan and Hedrich in their 1998 article, the new librarian should be shown the office, where supplies are kept, and where the break room is located, and during the training period, meetings should be set up for the new librarian to meet the other department heads.[14] The first morning on the job, the new librarian had an orientation session. He was given keys to his office and the building, his phone number, the code for long-distance calls, and introduction and access to file materials and supplies. Time with the book-keeper was spent discussing daily routines. A schedule and reference policy manual were left on his desk to go over prior to the first meeting with his mentor.

The new librarian would meet with the library dean beginning at half past ten, followed by a campus tour with a university staff member. After lunch, the protégé would begin his reference desk odyssey by shadowing me, the mentoring librarian, during my scheduled time. This allowed the new librarian to learn more about reference and the type of questions asked by students at Regent University. The first day concluded with a brief reintroduction to the library staff.

The remainder of the first week was devoted to

- time in technical services;
- time in access services;
- time to attend various library meetings;
- time to shadow at the reference desk; and
- an overview of liaison work with the various schools.

In technical services, the librarian was introduced to and given an overview of acquisitions, cataloging, and periodicals. In addition, the approval plan with Yankee Book Peddler and the William Tyndale College collection were discussed. Subject librarians at Regent University Library selected which books will be retained. Because of the volume of duplicate and unwanted titles, the library decided to hold a semiannual book sale.

> *During the training period, meetings should be set up for the new librarian to meet the other department heads.*

The sale helped the library handle all discards from both Tyndale and weeded titles from our collection. Later in the training, I further discussed collection development with the new librarian in more detail.

Meetings included one that dealt with the customer satisfaction survey and another on reference. The reference meeting had discussion regarding changing the virtual reference service that the library used. The service was not working for us; the program was clunky and patrons were not using it. The new librarian suggested that reference services try instant messaging (IM). Several librarians liked the idea and wanted to explore it further. Questions arose regarding implementation, and the new librarian answered them all. His experience with technology aided Regent University Library in setting up IM at both the reference desk and individual librarians' offices.

During the time with the head of access services, the protégé was given an overview of circulation and interlibrary loan operations. The protégé and I discussed problems and any questions or concerns he had. The new librarian began spending time with the reference and liaison librarians to learn about the various schools and library services. Time was set aside for the new librarian to become acquainted with the library and university web pages, which gave an in-depth perspective of the university, the library services, and where to locate needed information. He was given a series of questions to answer regarding the university web pages, particularly those of the library. For instance, one question asked where on the university web pages a student could go to put money on his or her print account. This type of question enables learners to quickly find answers to commonly asked questions. At times, the new librarian was assigned small jobs like obtaining his university identification card.

Job-specific discussion began toward the end of the first week. Top priority was his appointment as liaison to the School of Communication and the Arts. This designation entailed learning about course offerings and the vital resources brought into play for library instruction and collection development. Arrangements were made for the two of us to attend the next faculty meeting, September 2006. After being introduced by the school's dean, the librarian provided a short biography of himself and discussed services he could provide the faculty members and for the school.

The remaining schedule had the new librarian spending time

- learning about special collections;
- meeting the remaining subject specialists and learning about various resources;
- attending several new-student orientations with various librarians;
- going to a faculty retreat; and
- traveling to the D.C. campus for a new-student orientation.

James G. Rhoades and Arianne Hartsell, in a 2008 article, point out that orientations are a way for students to adjust to college life: "Becoming familiar with university resources like the library is one way students adjust to university life."[15] This helps students learn about library resources and improve research skills.[16] Early in the history of the college, the library at Regent University saw the benefits of having the librarian attend new student orientations. Librarians have been included in the various school orientations for a number of years. Earlier in the week, prior to the new-student orientation, the two of us sat and discussed what would be included in the presentation. We developed a handout for the students with the librarian's name and contact information along with important information regarding the library course, relevant databases, and other information. The library course is a required course for all students except for law. The course is online, is taken as a pass-fail course, and is self-paced. I began the orientation with a welcome and introduced myself and the newly hired librarian, who would assist them. Then the new librarian took over the orientation.

The new librarian and I traveled together to the satellite campus in the Washington, D.C., area for an orientation. I managed library services for the satellite campus from its inception in 2001 to its closure in 2008. The new student orientation was set for a Saturday morning, and it was scheduled to run

> in four one-hour blocks of time, beginning at 9 a.m. and ending at 1 p.m. The new students were divided into four groups and rotated to each of the four areas providing students with needed information. The new librarian set the laptop up next to the projector and managed the sequence of respective web pages as the head of reference talked about library services.[17]

Having a tech-savvy librarian helped me because I had no experience hooking up the projector to the laptop. The new librarian was a quick learner and was able to handle the fourth session of the orientation. After the session was over, we had lunch with the satellite campus staff member who assists me. During the trip back to the main campus, in Virginia Beach, the two of us discussed library-related issues. The discussion assisted the new librarian with settling into his new position.

After the two-week intense training period, I gave the new librarian time so he could complete assigned work. Mentoring continued as he had questions in regard to acting as the coordinator of the web team, doing liaison work, and being a member of the instruction and reference teams. He continued shadowing other librarians at the reference desk for another two to three weeks until he felt comfortable being alone at the desk. As pointed out by Weingart, Kochan, and Hedrich, "Additional tasks [are] added as the employee masters previous tasks."[18] After the training period, the new librarian was given three shifts on the reference desk. Hours for these shifts could be from nine to noon, noon to three, three to six, or six to ten. However, the librarians have a standing rule that new librarians are not assigned an evening shift during their first semester. Having only day hours means that other librarians are available to provide assistance. By late September of 2006, the new librarian was scheduled for the following shifts, which lasted until the end of the semester:

- Tuesday afternoons from three to six
- Thursday mornings from nine to noon
- Friday mornings from nine to noon

Each semester the reference schedule changes. At the time, six reference librarians staffed the reference desk Monday through Thursday evenings. Four librarians would each work one evening, six to ten, while two librarians had evenings off for the semester; thus, each librarian would have approximately ten desk hours a week. This related to the spring and fall semesters only, as evenings are not worked by librarians during the summer semester. The desk is not staffed during summer evening hours. During the mentoring process, it was pointed out that it helped knowing that an advocate was there to provide support and reassurance when mistakes were made during the learning process.

According to McKenzie, "Librarians need to know and understand about both sides of the library [Public Services and Technical Services], even if they only plan to work one side or the other."[19] Having experience only in systems made this new librarian aware of what was not working correctly within the system.

The new librarian was a wonderful asset to Regent University Library. Learning quickly, he was able to assume full responsibility for the School of Communications and the Arts, which included collection development. In addition, he was able to undertake the position of coordinator of the web team from the systems librarian, and he became an integral part of the reference and instruction teams. The mentoring relationship officially ended by the end of October, but a deep friendship has continued. During the 2007–2008 academic year, we decided to combine the instruction and reference teams officially as all six members were on both teams. During the spring and fall, we met twice a month for an hour. Each would chair the portion of the meeting he or she was responsible for: reference or instruction. Twice-monthly meetings enabled the librarians to keep up to date on items dealing with instruction and reference and to assist in making decisions on what we, as reference librarians, handle on a daily basis.

Not every library has an ethos that would support a mentorship program, and even if such an environment does exist, not every librarian is cut out to be a mentor depending on their personality and work styles.

Now an associate librarian at the University of Nebraska Kearney, my former colleague points out that "not every library has an ethos that would support a mentorship program, and even if such an environment does exist, not every librarian is cut out to be a mentor depending on their personality and work styles. Where it is possible for leadership to promote and receive buy-in from established library faculty, this has tremendous benefits in promoting morale and longevity in the workplace."[20]

Case Study Two: A University Library New Hire

During the spring of 2007, the liaison to the School of Psychology and Counseling gave notice that she would be leaving the end of June. Two individuals on campus expressed interest in the position; both individuals have their library degree. After discussion, the librarians decided to interview one of them, the cataloging librarian at the Regent University Law Library. She was working on a subject master's in the field of business administration with a concentration in marketing. The library dean planned on changing part of the job description of this position to include marketing. The candidate was brought in for an interview and subsequently offered the position of reference librarian. She would work at marketing the library, become the liaison to the School of Psychology and Counseling, assume reference duty, and work on other assignments. Her cataloging experience would be of benefit in her new position as a reference librarian.

Again, as the head of reference, I was assigned to mentor the new reference librarian. Her familiarity with the university made training her somewhat different and easier. However, she, like the previous librarian, needed extra assistance in being brought up to speed regarding reference, becoming a liaison to a school, and handling subject-specific collection development. A work schedule similar to the one for the librarian hired the year before, but shorter, was determined for the new librarian.

For the first work day in the library, in July 2007, I had the librarian spend time with the library bookkeeper to obtain office keys, to have her phone number transferred from the law library to her current office, and to be shown where supplies and file materials are kept. As with the previous librarian, I left a reference policy manual on her desk along with her training schedule for the training period. The first week schedule included

- time with the library dean;
- time for a library tour and introduction to staff;
- time with the instructional design librarian to learn about the required library course and library instruction needs;
- time with the technical and access services librarians;

- time at the reference desk shadowing other librarians;
- time learning about the various resources used; and
- time with the various liaison librarians learning about the schools and ways to answer questions.

The instructional design librarian provided her access to the course, asking her to review each lesson to understand what we expect students to know and to complete. This would help her to field questions regarding the course. The remaining portion of the afternoon was spent exploring the library web pages and familiarizing herself with the services provided.

Time in technical services was similar to the librarian's experience the year before, but her experience in technical services for twenty years made this session easier. The head of technical services and the protégé reviewed collection development and the Yankee Book Peddler approval plan. Time in access services gave the new librarian information on the operations of circulation and interlibrary loan. The service is similar to how the law library handles the two operations but on a larger scale. Having worked only in technical services, the protégé was not intimately informed about the services. The other component to access services is reference, wherein both of the librarians received more training than just an overview as it would be a large part of their job.

Time on the reference desk was scheduled for the new librarian with me and several other reference librarians. It is imperative to observe how several librarians handle reference at an institution to gain a broader view. Information provided to the new hire included user name and passwords for the reference computers, where to get replacement paper for the copiers and for printing, and where to gain assistance for the copiers. As with the previous librarian training, time was given for the new librarian to work in her office to learn more about the library web pages and to become familiar with the databases.

> *The instructional design librarian provided her access to the course, asking her to review each lesson to understand what we expect students to know and to complete.*

It is vital to make yourself available for any newly hired staff but even more so for librarians. Librarians handle the day-to-day operations of the library so must be given appropriate instruction and access to the individual who can provide the correct answer. Let's be honest about providing answers to staff members or for anyone. We do not have the answer for everything. So it is important to state "I am not sure, but I will find the answer"; people appreciate the honesty. Furthermore, they will know that you are on their side and will provide them truthful answers.

The protégé and I spent time each day reflecting on and evaluating library issues, most specifically reference-related issues.

This librarian began work in July, so the "training" period was not as rushed (as it had been a year earlier with the first librarian). In addition, I mainly concentrated on the reference aspects of the position as opposed to such busywork as filling out forms or securing identification cards. I am positive that both new librarians were happy to see the end of the first week of training. Most people would agree that the first week on a new job can be stressful, and often the individual feels that he or she is never going to learn the job. There appears to be so much information to absorb that it can seem overwhelming. However, as most people know, the job does get easier as the individual becomes better acquainted with a new position.

The second week of training the protégé librarian included

- further reviewing of web pages;
- reviewing syllabi from psychology and counseling courses;
- more shadowing of various librarians at the reference desk; and
- being primed on the marketing aspect of the position from the library dean.

The newly hired librarian was also instructed in the use of *Macromedia Dreamweaver,* the program we use for designing web pages. At the time, each librarian was responsible for maintaining library web pages in his or her respective subject areas; hers would be psychology and counseling.

The various school orientations were held in late August. For the psychology and counseling orientation, I made the handouts in PowerPoint in discussion with the new librarian. It centered on her understanding the contents of the presentation. Her contact information was included on the handout. She did not travel with me to handle the orientation at the satellite campus as it conflicted with other responsibilities.

At the end of August the annual faculty retreat was held just before classes began. I introduced the new librarian to the dean of the School of Psychology and Counseling during the first evening of the retreat. The two spent a few moments talking and getting to know each other. (Later in the semester, the dean invited the new liaison to attend a faculty meeting so they could get to know her.) Similar to the first librarian, this librarian would not have to do an evening shift on the reference desk the first semester. When she was comfortable with managing the reference desk solo, I provided her with her own set of desk hours. She began solo shifts the first week of the fall semester. Her shifts included

- Wednesday mornings from nine to noon;
- Thursday afternoons from noon to three; and
- Friday mornings from nine to one.

I would come to the desk to assist her with any questions she was unsure of how to answer; plus, the other reference librarians would help her. The evening reference schedule for the protégé was set in motion during her second semester as a part of the reference team. Any reference librarian will tell you that you might be a subject specialist, but when you are on the reference desk, you are a generalist. You can never anticipate the types of questions asked and need to prepare to assist in locating the information needed. If you are unable to fully answer the question, then librarian's business cards should be given to the patron with the idea to contact the liaison for further assistance.

Once trained, the new librarian has developed and grown into a wonderful asset to the reference team. She has been proactive in contacting the faculty of psychology and counseling regarding library services. Furthermore, marketing needs to take place so communities can become cognizant of the services and materials the library provides. As the marketing librarian, she is involved with all the special events within the university library. Since she began work, the librarian has been instrumental with special programs that include the Big Read, Constitution Day, new faculty teas, National Library Week, book sales, and the silver anniversary of the library.

Mentoring a newly hired librarian can be hard, time-consuming work, but after it is over, one continues to reap its rewards. The two librarians mentored during 2006 and 2007 have become friends and wonderful colleagues. They still consult with me regarding library issues or problems they encounter. Setting up a schedule that provides time for the gathered information to be integrated into their knowledge base was a benefit to both. Plus, both librarians stated that shadowing the other librarians at the reference desk helped them become familiar with the reference area, and the background in systems and technical services helped them provide reference services.

Mentoring relationships may result in writing collaboration between two or more librarians. "Most librarians do not have any release time for research or writing," notes Betsy McKenzie. [21] She further states that if the librarian has tenure at the university, then he or she tends to have release time for writing, but understanding that the librarian might not have release time "may help faculty members value writing done by librarians." [22] Collaborating in writing can be tough, but if one takes the lead to provide the article with one voice it can be done. Any librarian who has written with one or more colleagues can tell you it is possible and rewarding. It means not having to research and write an entire article alone.

Mentoring librarians in the workplace has engendered great satisfaction in knowing that I am helping someone build his or her career in providing guidance. Mentoring coworkers can provide one with a renewal of professional purpose. It can give one a sense of satisfaction of helping "influence the future of the profession [and the] ability to identify and advise."[23] The new librarians have also been a great asset in bestowing a grounding in what I do not know and what new things I must learn. The librarian hired in 2006 provided me enough confidence to become more technology savvy. He left Regent University in December 2009 to take a position at a university in Nebraska. We have stayed in touch and have written articles together. The newest hire, in 2007, and I have developed a friendship and value each other opinions. Having someone in the office to bounce ideas off of is a great help especially when developing instructional guides, web tutorials, or new services.

NOTES

1. Gail Munde, "Beyond Mentoring: Toward the Rejuvenation of Academic Libraries," *Journal of Academic Librarianship* 26, no. 3 (May 2000): 72.
2. Ibid.
3. Betsy McKenzie, "Why do Librarians Eat Their Young? And How Law Librarians Can Make Things Better," *The One Person Library* 25, no. 5 (September 2008): 8.
4. Janet Martorana, Eunice Schoeder, Lucia Snowhill, and Andrea L. Duda, "A Focus on Mentorship in Career Development," *Library Administration and Management* 18, no. 4 (Fall 2003): 198.
5. Marta Lee, "Growing Librarians: Mentorship in an Academic Library," *Library Leadership and Management* 23, no. 1 (Winter 2009): 34.
6. Martorana et al., 198.
7. Ibid., 201.
8. Tara Lynn Fulton, "Mentor Meets Telemachus: The Role of the Department Head in Orienting and Inducting the Beginning Reference Librarian," *Reference Librarian* 22, no. 26 (1990): 260.
9. Ibid., 266.
10. Ibid.
11. Sandra J. Weingart, Carol A. Kochan, and Anne Hedrich, "Safeguarding Your Investment: Effective Orientation for New Employees," *Library Administration and Management* 12, no. 3 (Summer 1998):156–58, HTML document.
12. Ibid.
13. Lee, 34.
14. Weingart, Kochan, and Hedrich, HTML document.

15. James G. Rhoades and Arianne Hartsell, "Marketing First Impressions: Academic Libraries Creating Partnerships and Connections at New Student Orientations," *Library Philosophy and Practice* (August 2008): 1.

16. Ibid.

17. Lee, 34.

18. Weingart, Kochan, and Hedrich, HTML document.

19. McKenzie, 8.

20. E-mail correspondence with Jon Ritterbush, associate librarian at University of Nebraska, Kearney, May 9, 2009.

21. McKenzie, 9.

22. Ibid.

23. Munde, 72.

SIX

MENTORING FOR PROMOTION

U p to this point, discussion has centered on mentoring library school students as interns to complete course assignments, mentoring potential students in deciding whether to attend library school, and the development of newly hired librarians in the workplace. This chapter will concentrate on the mentoring of coworkers in the promotion process in an academic setting. As mentioned previously, mentoring programs have been implemented to assist orienting new staff members to the institution.

Regent University provides basic orientations to bring workers up to speed with the institution's benefits and culture along with a tour of the campus. The library's provision of mentoring and job training help the new hire to adjust to the position. Training may be difficult, as each position has unique components associated with the job description. Parts of the job might be similar, but other parts can be dramatically different. For instance, training reference librarians might include how to deal with marketing or the handling of digital resources. Further, liaison work can be the same but different in that you are dealing with several people in the various subject areas.

Mentoring can assist librarians "with career planning advice, professional development guidelines, midcareer evaluation guidance, [and] personal development suggestions"[1] Following the period of a librarian's introduction to the library is a natural time for the mentor to continue being a source of advice, information, and suggestions. However, keep in mind that the mentor should not be perceived as the decision maker for the associate nor be readily available twenty-four hours a day.[2] In a 2008 article, Michele Crump, Carol Drum, and Colleen Seale state that there is much written regarding "the mentoring role in fostering professional development and helping untenured librarians successfully navigate through the tenure and promotion" process.[3] Not all academic librarians are tenured but most go through some type of promotion process. Good mentoring programs for promotion share common characteristics but "many programs have some distinguishing aspects that address individual needs or situations."[4] Addressing the individual needs of each library and librarian adds layers to each program. This can be a good thing as no one program works for every library or individual. Setting up mentoring programs for promotion demonstrates an institution's commitment to creating equal opportunity for all librarians.[5]

> *Many institutions have promotion mentoring programs that involve a six-month to one-year process. Preparing the dossier and professional activities are the main concentrations during this process.*

MENTORING PROGRAMS

Many institutions have promotion mentoring programs that involve a six-month to one-year process. Preparing the dossier and professional activities are the main concentrations during this process.[6] Concentrating on professional activities such as committee work, writing, and presentations are basic to the promotion. Being active professionally constitutes being on a committee through one's professional organization, grading advanced-placement exams, or providing guidance to individuals in one's subject area. Many universities have librarians pursuing tenure, so it is important to introduce new librarians to a research agenda and to involve them in professional activities early in their careers.[7] At other schools, like Pennsylvania State University (PSU), newly hired librarians are on the faculty tenure track[8] so expectations are that the librarian will be actively involved in scholarship (publication), teaching, and professional participation librarianship.[9] According to Bonnie Osif, PSU librarians are given a mentor for the first two years.[10]

PROMOTION GUIDELINES

In *Coaching in the Library,* Ruth Metz states that "mentoring is guidance from someone who has gone before."[11] So when guiding someone in attaining promotion, the expectation is that the "mentor [will have] experience, knowledge, and contacts that can help a particular individual achieve a specific goal."[12] Osif states that "faculty status and rank issues differ from one university to another, evaluation criteria vary, and career path options vary among institutions and individuals."[13] Even though criteria vary from institution to institution, Association of College and Research Libraries (ACRL) has guidelines for appointment, promotion, and tenure for cases where librarians have faculty status.[14] The ACRL guidelines for promotion state that the librarian should "perform professional level tasks that contribute to the educational level tasks that contribute to the educational and research mission of the institution."[15] ACRL points out that evidence for promotion may also be obtained from organizing or teaching workshops, contributing to the advancement of the profession, and conducting research.[16] Research may include publishing in scholarly journals, presentations, and grant writing. The ACRL guidelines for promotion also state that movement to the specific rank of assistant, associate, or full librarian means having a successful record of teaching, advancement of the profession, and publishing, beginning at the lower rank. For example, the guidelines for assistant professor state that "promotion to this rank shall require evidence of significant professional contributions to the library or the institution."[17] This can often be difficult to achieve, as many librarians are new to the field when entering the workforce as an assistant librarian. The guidelines also discuss the procedures that should be addressed when considering a librarian for promotion to associate or full librarian.[18]

A difficult part of the promotion process is in defining what "advancement of the profession" or professional service really means. Professional service has been defined as "activities such as participating or holding office in professional associations and societies."[19] It has been argued that standards for librarians should be consistent to those for teaching faculty. However, service criteria are often vague and do not offer much assistance in defining service and what is acceptable in the way of service. Surveys have stated that activities considered service include being members of university and national committees and participating in religious and civic activities.[20] Many universities apply different weights to various levels of service. These levels range from being a member of a national committee to chairing the committee to "holding officer positions at the organization level."[21] Service can mean being an active member on a national committee.

However, service raises the question of how much weight it will carry for tenure or promotion. How much weight does it have compared to other requirements, such as publication?[22] Service is not as tough as it sounds. It can mean that a librarian just commits to attending national conferences for a certain amount of time and becomes an active participant. Joining a national committee is as simple as filling out volunteer forms with your professional organizations. Both ALA and ACRL have online access to volunteer forms; often the forms are online and interactive, and they may be submitted electronically. "Serving actively and effectively on a library or a university committee" means saying yes when appointed to the committee (can you realistically say no?).[23]

Service is hard to define, and there is no easy answer, but it is expected as part of the promotion process. Find out what is acceptable regarding service at your institution, and make it a priority to include it in your daily work activities. Academic reference librarians may have multiple demands on their time when pursuing promotion or tenure, including completing their regular responsibilities as a librarian.[24] It can be tough to continue working a full load while striving to fulfill tenure or promotion requirements.[25] Full loads or regular responsibilities often include spending time on the reference desk, being a liaison to an academic department or school (or often multiple schools), handling collection development, conducting instruction, serving on library and university committees, and many other responsibilities. Conducting research and writing for peer-reviewed publications to gain promotion can be a struggle for librarians because "most librarians do not have release time for research or writing."[26] In a 2007 article, Todd Spires points out that many of the duties librarians perform on a daily basis involve a great amount of time. He includes many of those already mentioned above but also includes answering e-mails from students and faculty, providing formal and informal instruction sessions, and supervising students or library personnel.

> *The ACRL guidelines for promotion state that the librarian should "perform professional level tasks that contribute to the educational level tasks that contribute to the educational and research mission of the institution."*

To obtain tenure or promotion these librarians are required to publish, give presentations, acquire a second master's degree, and be active within professional organizations.[27]

Case Study: Promotions at Regent University library

At Regent University Library, librarians are not given release time to do research, to write scholarly articles, to prepare for presentations, or to write grants. Often librarians conduct some research during their time on the reference desk. Articles on their topic can be located, printed, stapled, and set aside to address patron questions and needs. Regent University librarians are not tenured but have faculty status and pursue promotion. Faculty status at a university means that librarians are expected to be actively involved with professional activities, give presentations, write for publication, and "provide effective librarianship."[28] Most of the Regent University Library librarians are members of American Library Association

> *Conducting research and writing for peer-reviewed publications in order to gain promotion can be a struggle for librarians because "most librarians do not have release time for research or writing."*

(ALA), Association of Christian Librarians (ACL), or American Theological Library Association (ATLA). Five of the eight librarians are active committee members on various committees of ALA and ACL. For example, I have been an active member of the Research Committee (2004–2009) that is part of the Distance Learning section of ACRL; ACRL membership means that first you have to be a member of ALA. In the past, the Research Committee has worked at providing mentoring to librarians who were preparing professional presentations, submitting proposals, and writing for publication.

One year the Research Committee that I serve on took on the responsibility of being the Presentation Committee for the distance-learning section. Each year the distance-learning section has a workshop or gives presentation at the ALA Annual Conference so the committees rotate the responsibility for the presentation or workshop. The Research Committee gave a presentation on editing scholarly manuscripts for publication at the 2007 annual meeting of ALA. The following spring, several members of the committee did a writing workshop at the Off Campus Library Services Conference in Salt Lake City, Utah.

Being active on committees within your professional membership provides opportunities to be part of a presentation without doing the entire project solo. It can also provide the opportunity to come home with ideas for providing new services, opportunities for mentoring others,

> *In the past, the Research Committee has worked at providing mentoring to librarians who were preparing professional presentations, submitting proposals, and writing for publication.*

or perhaps writing an article. Attending several of the off campus conferences has meant that I brought back ideas for our satellite campus. In addition, this engendered enough confidence for me to write and publish. Being active in ALA and getting published helped me to get promoted from assistant to associate librarian in 2006. Since then, I mentored two librarians desiring to go up for promotion during the 2006–2007 academic year.

A common theme running though the library literature regarding promotion and tenure is that many academic librarians are extremely busy at work and are active in their personal lives. Finding the necessary time to do all that is needed for promotion or tenure can overwhelm anyone. Tenure requires providing effective librarianship in the workplace, conducting research that can result in publication, and being active professionally, which may seem daunting. Spires, as others have, questions "what the appropriate mix of librarianship, scholarship and service" is for promotion.[29] What is the appropriate mix for the academic librarian? Should a time frame be considered? Answering these questions can be extremely difficult, especially when some librarians might be accomplishing all three aspects, whereas others might have completed only one or two aspects. Another aspect to consider is which is more important. Librarians have their regular workload to complete as well. The one or two aspects completed by some librarians might be enough to be granted promotion.

> Librarians "should contribute to the university by: serving actively and effectively on library and university committees; seeking opportunities to represent the university in community service based on their expertise; and assuming leadership roles in professional organizations."

Regent University librarians are required to fulfill certain requirements for promotion consideration. One example in the promotion of assistant to associate is that the librarian "should have a minimum of three years of full-time library experience."[30] Some individuals think that the quality of experience should be at the school in which the librarian is seeking the promotion. Other individuals differ in that the quality of experience exceeds place of service in importance. The librarians "should demonstrate excellence in the performance of their duties."[31] Evidence for performing excellence in their jobs will be through the yearly evaluations with consistently moderate to high overall ratings; the dean of the library will determine the evaluation instrument utilized.[32]

Regent University's *Faculty and Academic Policy Handbook* asserts that the librarians should demonstrate productivity in research and scholarly or creative activity, evidence of which may include: submitting original contributions in professional journals; contributing research that is presented in professional conferences or seminars; authoring or coauthoring published books; and submitting other forms of research and scholarly or creative activity for professional presentation or distribution.[33]

It further maintains that librarians "should contribute to the university by: serving actively and effectively on library and university committees; seeking opportunities to represent the university in community service based on their expertise; and assuming leadership roles in professional organizations."[34] Many academic institutions recognize that being active in "professional service activities had beneficial effects for the individual, the institution, and the profession as a whole."[35]

To assist the librarians seeking promotions, I consulted the *Faculty and Academic Policy Handbook* for the promotion review timetable (see appendix E). Then a schedule was established for both librarians to follow in assembling their promotion dossier. The timetable kept them on track for submission to the library dean on the first of November.

Prior to beginning work mid-August 2006, the new librarian was contacted via e-mail. He was instructed to bring everything that he had completed over the years as a professional librarian while working at other libraries. We would review the materials to decide what would be most useful for his promotion dossier. The other librarian seeking promotion was also instructed to gather everything she had that would assist in the promotion process. The two protégés and the managing librarian met for lunch on the last Friday in August to discuss the promotion process and the dossiers. The librarians were then given the promotion schedule. The "Outline for Faculty Tenure and Promotion Dossier" (which can be found online, at www.regent.edu/ academics/academic_affairs/faculty_handbook.cfm#outline_dossier) is broken into five parts, and the promotion schedule allowed one week for each part.

After the first meeting, the three of us met once a week; I would review documents and answer questions. The "schedule aided in keeping the librarians on track while completing their dossier [in addition to] their regular workload."[36]

When gathering materials, the librarians were instructed to include a narrative regarding the accomplishments wherever relevant. The narratives would be placed in the front of the dossier with supporting documents in appendixes. The narrative might look something like this:

> The Collection Development has been accomplished through consultation of bibliographies, *Books in Print,* the yellow slips from Yankee Book Peddler, publisher flyers, and faculty members (Appendix II A 1). This past year the library acquired the collection from Tyndale College. Materials from Tyndale are evaluated for appropriateness to the Regent University collection.[37]

The extract above is from my dossier. Corresponding materials in the appendix included correspondence between the government faculty and me dealing with ordering relevant material.

The two librarians were allowed to review my dossier as they compiled their own. As their mentor, I reviewed their narratives and accompanying documents. The dossiers were due to the library dean on the first of November; the dean would pass them onto the Promotion Committee. Promotion committees are made up of three faculty members; the members may include associate librarians, full librarians, associate professors, or full professors. For a librarian pursuing full librarianship, the three-member committee has only full librarians or full professors. At the time, the library had two full librarians and three associate librarians available to serve on the two promotion committees for associate librarian.

Four librarians would be part of the two promotion committees; two librarians would be on each committee along with one faculty member from the school where the librarian was the liaison. For the new librarian, a faculty member from the School of Communications and the Arts agreed to participate. A faculty member from the School of Psychology and Counseling agreed to sit on the other librarian's promotion committee. Each committee had a librarian as the chair of the committee who would make sure other committee members reviewed the dossier. The committee chair would take the comments from the other committee members and write a letter of support or nonsupport of the promotion. In both cases, the librarians received supporting letters for their promotions from their committees; the promotion packages, which included the dossiers, were given to the library dean for consideration. The dean would write a letter of support or nonsupport, as appropriate, and forward the dossiers to the university provost for consideration. Promotions are announced at an all-staff meeting after the annual board meeting in April.

After the dossiers were returned to the library dean with support for both librarians being promoted, the librarian who was the liaison for the School of Psychology and Counseling decided to return to Greece so she withdrew her promotion request. According to the *Faculty and Academic Policy Handbook,* a "candidate may withdraw her/his tenure or promotion application at any stage of the process."[38] The dossier was given back to her. The remaining librarian received notification of promotion at the all-staff meeting in May; the promotion took effect on the first of July 2007.

During late spring of 2008, I was approached again to mentor another librarian who sought the rank of associate librarian. I used the promotion schedule from the other two librarians as a template; I changed the dates to reflect the time period. The two of us met to discuss the promotion process and expectations. Upon receipt of the schedule, he and I discussed the importance of staying on schedule due to his full workload. As with the other promotion mentoring, the two of us would meet once a week to review his progress.

Not only was there the normal workload but he was the principal contact person for a Big Read grant; this grant resulted in an extremely busy time for him. I knew the Big Read was going to consume much of his time, and I needed to tell him that there was nothing wrong in waiting a year. He would make an excellent associate librarian, but as a good mentor I had to be honest in stating that lack of sufficient time could factor into his not completing the dossier on schedule. However, he maintained that he could handle the work-

> *Not only was there the normal workload but he was the principal contact person for a Big Read grant; this grant resulted in an extremely busy time for him.*

load and wanted to continue. Because of the extra workload, the librarian had trouble meeting the schedule deadlines. I told him I was there to help, but ultimately he needed to get the work finished if he still wanted to be promoted. A final deadline was given if he wanted me to review the completed dossier before submission to the library dean and promotion committee. The deadline passed without a completed dossier. He gave it to me several days later. I told him that I would review it but would not have enough time to give it my undivided attention. I did a quick review, made a few suggestions, and returned it. At the May all staff meeting it was announced that the librarian made promotion, taking effect July 2009.

Mentoring coworkers for promotion does not mean a long-term commitment on the part of the mentor. As noted above, some academic libraries provide mentoring programs for those seeking promotion that can involve a six-month to one-year process. At Regent University, library faculty are encouraged from day one to become active in their field, give presentations, conduct research, pursue scholarly publishing, and provide service at the university and off campus. So mentoring someone for promotion does not mean a year or more commitment. Mentoring for promotion can be conducted in as little as seven to eight weeks, which includes preparation time and time to critique the dossier prior to submission.

Regent University librarians are also encouraged to maintain a yearly folder. The folder is for keeping records of faculty meeting attendance for the school, instruction presentations, and so forth. At the year's end, when librarians are itemizing accomplishments, the folder is useful. It also helps when the individual is pursuing promotion, as it is difficult and almost impossible to remember what you did five years ago or even last year. Since starting work here more than nine years ago, I began filing handouts from orientations and workshops in the folder.

> *Remember that every time you get an article published, you serve on a committee, or you mentor someone, it adds to your next dossier.*

Besides placing items in a physical folder, I have placed notes in the various e-mail folders stating what I did for the faculty for the School of Government or the other schools I worked with over the years. This provides documentation of what was completed and makes it easier when I go up for promotion.

The file is a great place for all completed or in-process jobs. This includes dated draft copies of articles sent to a publisher. It may be a record of what did not get published, but I was writing and this took time. Not every article will get accepted, so do not take it personally; just keep trying. Remember that every time you get an article published, you serve on a committee, or you mentor someone, it adds to your next dossier. You are also helping another individual build his or her dossier, even if it happens not to be in the library field. For me, the most important aspect of mentoring has been the satisfaction of knowing that I helped others, even a little bit, along their road of life. You never know when you might need a hand up along the way. A little kindness will be returned to you tenfold.

NOTES

1. Judith Field, "Mentoring: A Natural Act for Information Professionals?" *New Library World* 102, no. 1166/1167 (2001): 270.
2. Ibid.
3. Michele Crump, Carol Drum, and Colleen Seale, "Establishing a Pre-tenure Review Program in an Academic Library," *Library Administration and Management* 22, no. 1 (Winter 2008): 1.

4. Ibid.

5. Field, 269.

6. Crump et al., 3.

7. Crump et al., 4.

8. Bonnie Osif, "Successful Mentoring Program: Examples from Within and Without the Academy," *Journal of Business and Finance Librarianship* 13, no. 3 (2008): 338.

9. "Guideline UL-HRG07 Promotion and Tenure Criteria Guidelines," www .libraries.psu.edu/psul/jobs/facultyjobs/p_t_guidelines.html.

10. Osif, 338.

11. Ruth Metz, *Coaching in the Library* (Chicago: American Librarian Association, 2001), 8.

12. Ibid.

13. Osif, 336.

14. ACRL Committee on the Status of Academic Librarians, "A Guideline for the Appointment, Promotion, and Tenure of Academic Librarians," *College and Research Libraries News* 66, no. 9 (June 2005): 668.

15. Ibid., 670.

16. Ibid.

17. Ibid.

18. Ibid., 670–71.

19. Candace R. Benefiel, Jeannie P. Miller, Pixey Anne Mosley, and Wendie Arant-Kaspar, "Service to the Profession: Definitions, Scope, and Value," *Reference Librarian* 73 (2001): 364.

20. Ibid., 364–65.

21. Ibid., 366.

22. Ibid., 362.

23. *Faculty and Academic Policy Handbook,* www.regent.edu/academics/ academic_affairs/faculty_handbook.cfm#library_faculty.

24. Newkirk Barnes, "Doing It All: First Year Challenges for New Academic Reference Librarians," *The Reference Librarian* 47, no. 1 (2007): 51.

25. Ibid., 52.

26. Betsy McKenzie, "Why Do Librarians Eat Their Young? And How Law Librarians Can Make Things Better," *The One-Person Library* 25, no. 1 (September 2008): 9.

27. Todd Spires, "The Busy Librarian: Prioritizing Tenure and Dealing with Stress for Academic Library Professionals," *Illinois Libraries* 84, no. 4 (Spring 2007): 101.

28. Ibid., 102.

29. Ibid., 104.

30. *Faculty and Academic Policy Handbook.*

31. Ibid.

32. Ibid.

33. Ibid.

34. Ibid.
35. Benefiel et al., 362.
36. Marta Lee, "Growing Librarians: Mentorship in an Academic Library," *Library Leadership and Management* 23, no. 1 (Winter 2009): 35.
37. Dossier of Marta Lee; October 2005.
38. *Faculty and Academic Policy Handbook.*

SEVEN

VOLUNTEERS IN LIBRARIES AND LIBRARIANS AS VOLUNTEERS

Volunteers play vital roles in the daily operations of libraries. It has been stated that "the library belongs to our community and to everyone in it."[1] So it seems appropriate that the community should be involved in helping to operate the library. Historically, volunteers have provided many services that would not have occurred otherwise. For example, "Prior to the 1930s, volunteers provided many lending services, especially to the homesteaders of the West."[2] Without volunteers, libraries would not have continued to develop and expand around the world and especially in the United States. Over the years, the nature of volunteering "has not diminished the importance of volunteers," but the group of people who do the volunteering has changed.[3] In the past, volunteers were largely unemployed, middle-class housewives.

> *Historically, volunteers have provided many services that would not have occurred otherwise.*

Only about 10 percent of the volunteers fall into this category in recent years. Even with the change in the demographics of volunteers, Americans have continued to volunteer.[4]

VOLUNTEER DUTIES

A recent trend is to have volunteers help answer e-mail inquiries. The volunteers answer the questions that they are able to and leave the more difficult inquiries for the professional staff. Answering e-mails does not have to take place in the library but can be conducted from the volunteer's home through an Internet connection. "Volunteers can also help libraries continue provid[ing] a human touch that library users continue to need when using libraries' information retrieval systems."[5] Many businesses fail to provide either that human touch or effective customer service. The library continues to be contacted, states Erica Nicol and Corey M. Johnson, because a library is viewed as a "reliable human intermediary for information retrieval."[6]

It has been predicted that as online usage of libraries grows, the need for additional staff will increase. This can place additional stress on the library because of a shrinking or stagnant budget. Budgets often cannot take on the additional costs of a larger staff. Volunteers do not need to be

> *Many volunteer programs began during a library's time of financial difficulty.*

tech savvy; just the willingness to respond to patron questions can be enough. Volunteers with good reference questioning skills can refer the patron to print sources. Knowing and identifying the proper print source can relieve the patron from waiting for the online source to be available.

Often, the patron does not know what he or she really wants so it is helpful to ask questions about the topic. This leads to the correct information and relevant sources. For example, the undergraduates at Regent University are required to take a general course related to locating scholarly materials and research. The course syllabus brings the students into the library to locate information on postmodernism. The reference interview reveals that the student needs information on postmodernism in regard to sin or evil. Librarians introduce the student to *Academic Search Complete,* a general database that has proven fruitful for this topic. Highly trained reference volunteers or graduate assistants have been extremely helpful answering this type of question in an academic setting and especially at Regent University Library.

Many volunteer programs began during a library's time of financial difficulty. Nicol and Johnson contend that library services can suffer when volunteers replace professional staff. When this is done, the authors argue, the duties of paid and volunteer staff overlap, with volunteers performing essential services. What happens when the volunteer leaves? Plus, it makes it difficult to justify hiring more paid staff when finances are better. The authors further state that quality volunteer programs take time and money to operate. For example, volunteers need to be recruited, supervised, trained, and recognized.[7] It can be a problem when the library depends on volunteers to assist at service points. For example, York County Public Library, in Yorktown, Virginia, has scheduled volunteers at the public service desk only to have them not show up. When the director called to see where they were, they responded by saying that they were just volunteers and could come and go as they please.[8] However, a benefit of utilizing volunteers is that they provide many quality programs and services for the library. Volunteers operate reading programs for preschoolers in public libraries and often reshelve materials, which gives the paid staff time to assist patrons or to conduct other types of work.

Volunteers more often work in public libraries but play important roles in special, school, and academic libraries as well. Volunteers at schools help in the library or in the classroom; they might welcome those visiting a special library; volunteers can shelve and process books in technical services or handle a score of other jobs in academia. Public libraries utilize volunteers in various aspects of operating the library.

MENTORING VOLUNTEERS

Volunteers need direction as they complete assigned jobs in the workplace. Mentoring the volunteer is an opportunity to provide interesting jobs, or at least make the work appear to be appealing. This is important in that all tasks need to be completed and are vital for the library's operation. How does mentoring come into play in volunteer work? Nearly every work opportunity with volunteers offers a chance to be a mentor. Yet often volunteers have bestowed on me as much mentoring as I have given them; it is a two-way street. Two-way mentoring benefits both individuals involved. Remember that mentoring does not always mean the same thing in every situation. Mentoring volunteers is different than mentoring or supervising an internship for a library school student. Many volunteers have no official training in the library field, which can mean that they do not understand the big picture of library work. Volunteers often do not desire to handle certain jobs they feel are beneath them. However, any type of mentoring can benefit both the teacher and the student.

While in library school, I volunteered at the local public library to add experience to my résumé and to gain practice in the area of technical services. During this period, a paraprofessional cataloger worked with me, asking me to assist in the maintenance of the card catalog. When I worked at the catalog, patrons would ask me for assistance in locating materials or for suggestions on their topics, help I was able to give thanks to the paraprofessional's sharing her ideas and experiences with me. Moreover, the librarian, who managed the small-town library system, became a wonderful mentor for me in that I could ask her anything to do with libraries and get straight answers.

MENTORING PUBLIC LIBRARY VOLUNTEERS

Other public libraries use volunteers to assist with special projects, and mentoring is needed to teach the volunteers the necessary tasks. For example, a public library in Denver came up with a unique program involving disabled middle-school students. The librarian "posed the idea of having the teens do some simple volunteer tasks on their weekly visits, to channel their energy into a more focused direction."[9] Jobs that the students assisted with included alphanumeric sorting, tidying up the board books, collating handouts, and shelving materials. All the jobs made the student volunteers feel important, and they did jobs that the staff did not have to complete.[10] Another public library system has volunteers take reading materials to homebound seniors. This program is rapidly expanding, as the volunteers like the interaction with the seniors, and the seniors like the one-on-one interaction with the volunteers.[11]

> The librarian "posed the idea of having the teens do some simple volunteer tasks on their weekly visits, to channel their energy into a more focused direction."

A public library in Indiana utilizes teens as volunteers; this fosters good relations with the public. The Friends of the Library have collected donations to inaugurate a college-scholarship program that would reward the students for their hard work. In 2001, four students who worked in the library were granted $500 scholarships for college.[12] Some public libraries have special projects that are operated solely by volunteers. These projects include assisting the children's librarian with the story time for preschoolers; the volunteers are called the *Story Time Ladies*. This program is so popular that the library had to increase the number of story times per week. Another program has volunteers operating a "slightly used book store," which yields the library about twelve thousand dollars a year.[13] Many public libraries use volunteers to benefit the library and to provide the volunteer with a purpose.

York County Public Library utilizes volunteers to assist with many jobs. Ninety-five percent of the volunteers working in this public library system are willing to do various jobs that need to be completed. Even so, as Kevin Smith, director of York County Public Library, notes, "Volunteers are very enthusiastic about working for the library until the first day of work, when they [become] dismayed that [the library staff] do more than sit around and read books all day."[14] This can be a typical reaction of many individuals who have never thought about the day-to-day operations of a library prior to volunteering. These same volunteers are surprised to find that shelving books can be tedious. In addition, some volunteers are amazed to realize that while shelving books, they can encounter some rather unpleasant patrons.[15] Mentoring such individuals requires sharing with them some of the realities of library work and assuring them that many good times come along with the not-so-good times.

> *Volunteers are very enthusiastic about working for the library until the first day of work, when they [become] dismayed that [the library staff] do more than sit around and read books all day.*

Once York County Public Library had a volunteer who liked to clean and polish the books. Often the volunteer would be so involved with cleaning the books that patrons would be "delayed from leaving until all of the books were nice and shiny."[16] While shelving, the volunteer would clean books, so not many books could be reshelved. But volunteers at the York County Public Library system have implemented many successful programs and services. For example, the summer reading program could not be completed without the teen volunteers. One individual who is trained in repairing books enables the library to save money on binding and repairing of materials.[17]

While working at a public library system near Richmond, Virginia, Smith mentored a high-school-student library volunteer. The student went from volunteer to page to several different paid library positions and has now gone to library school to become a library professional. According to Smith, the experience of providing guidance to someone along his or her career path was very rewarding.[18] Plus, Smith's working with volunteers has been very rewarding, and he plans to continue.

MENTORING SCHOOL AND SPECIAL LIBRARY VOLUNTEERS

The media specialist delivers more than access to library materials; he or she is "also teacher, an instructional partner, and an information specialist."[19] The media specialist handles technology along with assisting every student who attends the school. Larger school systems have media specialists for each school but often have to rely on volunteers to help in the library. Schools that cannot afford a media specialist often depend on parents to volunteer in the library. Twenty years ago, as a school library volunteer, I managed the checkout process for all grades, from prekindergarten to eighth grade.

Special libraries rely on volunteers just as museums rely on docents. Docents give tours that might not occur if the museum had to rely on paid staff. Some docents or volunteers give their time because they enjoy the topic or history of the institution.

At the Mariners Museum in Newport News, Virginia, many of the volunteers and docents help in researching topics for museum displays. The volunteers utilize the museum's extensive library in their research. The library depends on volunteers to assist the archivist in processing and cataloging materials, researching projects, and answering patron requests. Mentoring in special libraries provides an opportunity to instruct others in administering quality service to the patron while presenting appropriate materials and teaching about a specialized area. Specialized areas might be about maritime history, law, or corporate issues.

MENTORING ACADEMIC LIBRARY VOLUNTEERS

Academic libraries also depend on volunteers to complete jobs. Regent University Library has depended on volunteers for a number of years, as noted in chapter 4.

In the fall of 2007, one potential MLS school student approached the library dean about the possibility of shadowing a librarian in order to explore the field as a possible career choice. The student met with me, the mentor, to discuss her interests. She was interested in reference as a career choice; this helped me set up projects for her. Times for her to come to the library were established along with scheduled time for her to meet with staff members. An overview of the library's operation gave her a better understanding of the library as a workplace.

After she spent time in each section of the library and with each librarian, she and I sat down to discuss librarianship as a profession. I even had her talk to the paraprofessionals in Circulation, Acquisitions, Periodicals, and Interlibrary Loan, as these jobs are usually supervised by a librarian. Librarians need to know how these jobs are completed in order to be a better librarian. Because the student had no library experience, I asked her if she had time to volunteer in any library. She did have time, and she volunteered in the library two half days per week. Any type of experience is better than having no library experience on a résumé when applying for a professional position, and this volunteer work would look impressive on her résumé. Because she was new to library work but wanted to be a librarian, I thought that it would be good for her to gain experience from the "bottom" up, so she began in Circulation, shelving, checking materials in and out, and assisting with other jobs.

After several weeks, we expanded her experience by adding labeling materials in Technical Services. The volunteer student was shown how to do the job so that she could work independently when she arrived. An important part of mentoring any individual is imparting the confidence to do a job, and do it well. Thus, in both departments, she was trained by supervisors who fully understood the work and could help her understand it—and enjoy it—as well. Both Circulation and Technical Services appreciated the extra help as the student assistant budget was cut in half.

Regent University Library has had one volunteer working in the library for more than ten years. After I was hired as a reference librarian, I was designated as the liaison to the School of Government. The volunteer, a retired government documents librarian, was asked to work with me and help me learn about call number ranges, among other topics. The volunteer mentored me on how things were accomplished by the previous government librarian and provided assistance on locating where various materials were kept. In addition, she helped with many projects and gave advice when asked for it. After I became acclimated to the library culture and the way things were completed in the library, the volunteer and I worked on many projects together.

> *Because she was new to library work but wanted to be a librarian, I thought that it would be good for her to gain experience from the "bottom" up.*

Within a month of my beginning work, I began putting a collection of materials from the 1988 presidential election in order and indexing the materials. The volunteer helped me sort the materials, including newspapers, which are a large part of the collection.

While the volunteer began sorting these newspapers, I began looking at the entire collection. At the time we started, a government student was working as a graduate assistant at the reference desk. The student was in the campaign-management track with the School of Government, so the project was of strong interest to him. Because he knew the subject matter well, I had him sort through the material, put like things together, and list the contents of each box. After each box, we would discuss what was there; I had the student tell me his ideas on the materials and how he put it together. Sometimes supervisors will find trainees with excellent skills and knowledge in other areas. As noted earlier, mentoring is often a two-way street, and the supervisor can learn much from the trainee. This was certainly the case here, and much information was shared during the project's long duration.

MENTORING LONG-TERM VOLUNTEERS

Working with a long-term volunteer or a volunteer program offers different challenges. For one thing, each day the volunteer comes to work, time needs to be taken by the supervisor to find out how things are going both with the job and at home (with volunteers, especially, home situations can affect work schedules and performance). As with all mentoring, be prepared for minor interruptions to answer questions or to address problems. Remember, the volunteer is giving up his or her time to aid the library; be sensitive to the volunteer's time, and find ways to show your appreciation. For example, each year around Regent University Library's long-term volunteer's birthday, I bring in cupcakes or cake and we celebrate. She takes the remaining cupcakes or cake and shares with the technical service staff. I do it this way because I know that she does not like public appreciations and that she can share with the staff on her terms.

Working with volunteers means planning ahead so that jobs are ready when the volunteer arrives at work. Plus, a certain amount of supervision by a staff member is necessary to ensure that the job is completed in a satisfactory way and in a specified amount of time. Decisions need to be made by a paid staff member, who will be responsible for the outcome. If supervising a volunteer takes a large amount of time, then it would probably be best to handle the job yourself instead. Some believe that it is important to maintain a quality program if the library goes ahead with volunteers. Quality programs involve having jobs for the volunteer to handle that are important to the library and not just busywork. However, the library can assign a full- or part-time staff member to manage the volunteer program.[20]

> *As with all mentoring, be prepared for minor interruptions to answer questions or to address problems. Remember, the volunteer is giving up his or her time to aid the library; be sensitive to the volunteer's time, and find ways to show your appreciation.*

Does the cost outweigh the benefits of volunteers? Certainly, there is a downside to working with volunteers. Some volunteers may not take the position seriously, which can mean dealing with their not showing up when they said that they would. This can be difficult when they are assigned to a service point, like the circulation desk. In addition, staff can be affected by the volunteer's idiosyncrasies (we had one volunteer who liked to clean the books with Goo-Gone). Even so, the benefits of working with volunteers outnumber the problems, so do not hesitate to work with a volunteer or start a volunteer program.

My experience with volunteers in an academic setting has meant spending a small amount of time thinking about the jobs that the volunteer can do for the library but receiving a great return. There are more jobs than I can ever conceive of completing, and with a bit of mentoring, volunteers can help. Having such help allows me to concentrate on the bigger picture and services.

NOTES

1. Erica Nicol and Corey M. Johnson, "Volunteers in the Library: Program Structure, Evaluation and Theoretical Analysis," *Reference and User Services Quarterly* 48, no. 2 (2008): 154.
2. Ibid.
3. Ibid., 155.
4. Ibid.
5. Ibid., 155–56.
6. Ibid., 155.
7. Ibid., 157.
8. E-mail correspondence with Kevin Smith, director of York County Public Library, August 5, 2009.
9. Emily Dagg, "Middle School Volunteers with Special Needs at the Denver Public Library," *Young Adult Library Services* (Summer 2006): 40.
10. Ibid., 41.
11. Jennifer T. Ries-Taggart, "Brighton Memorial Offers Reading Partnership with Seniors," *Public Libraries* 48, no. 1 (January/February 2009): 11–12.
12. Kay Shelton, "Starting a Volunteer Program in a Community College Library," *Community and Junior College Libraries* 14, no. 3 (2008): 171.
13. William E. Buchanan, "Volunteerism in Small and Rural Public Libraries in Pennsylvania," *Bookmobile and Outreach Services* 11, no. 2 (2008): n.p.
14. E-mail correspondence with Kevin Smith, director of York County Public Library, August 5, 2009.
15. Ibid.
16. Ibid.
17. Ibid.
18. Ibid.
19. Allison Kaplan, "Is Your School Librarian 'Highly Qualified'?" *Phi Delta Kappan* (December 2007): 301.
20. Nicol and. Johnson, 157.

EIGHT

MENTORING LIBRARIANS ELECTRONICALLY

A s stated in chapter 1, a mentor can be defined as one who advises, counsels, guides, or teaches others. Janet Hilbun and Lynn Akin affirm that "mentoring is a traditional method of passing knowledge and skills on from an established professional to a junior or new member of the field."[1] Technology has made our lives easier in the way of communicating with others with the use of e-mail, Facebook, and other programs. A natural consequence of electronic communication technology is that e-mentoring—that is, mentoring librarians electronically—has grown in importance.[2] E-mentoring provides the opportunity to assist new professionals in learning about the field. It can also help professionals who have been in the profession for a while but have taken on new responsibilities. In addition, the mentor and the protégé do not have to be at the same institution.

MENTORING AND ACADEMIC RESEARCH USING BITNET CONFERENCING TO ENCOURAGE RESEARCH

In 1991 a unique project called Mentoring and Academic Research using Bitnet conferencing to encourage research began at the American Library Association's Annual Conference, held in Atlanta, Georgia. The project's aim was to get more professionals involved in conducting research in the library field. Project participants were broken into six groups; each group would have one or more mentors, a facilitator, and a group of librarians. All participants would be at their home locations and participate through a discussion list, utilizing the e-mail system to send messages. "The electronic mentoring project attempted to extend the traditional practice of mentoring by creating small groups of mentors and protégés" interested in the same type of library research.[3]

Many of the participants grouped together would be from various institutions; none from the same institution would be in the same group. This gave the protégés the freedom to explore without worrying about repercussions in the workplace. Discussion resulted in the librarians being on equal footing as opposed to the hierarchy that is in place when mentoring in person. Furthermore, the electronic format allowed for thoughtful and meaningful responses (composing a message can be done at a slower pace), which often do not happen in "real life" discussions. However, written responses can be misconstrued and cause problems.[4] As with any project, this one also had difficulties to overcome such as technical problems and getting each group started. One of the groups decided to conduct research that one participating member wanted to explore in his library.[5] In all, many lessons were learned from this project, including training methods and responding when the facilitator is away for a time or switches jobs.

VIRTUAL MENTORING STUDIES

Virtual mentoring studies can be guided by the following:

1. The success of online mentoring depends on familiarity with all aspects of the program shared by material writers, tutors, mentors and assessors.

2. The success of online mentoring depends on the quality of the relationship that is established between mentor and learner.

3. The success of online mentoring depends on the degree of motivation the learner feels before and during mentoring.

4. The success of online mentoring depends on the participants' computer efficacy, including the adequacy of the hardware, software, and the Internet aspects for interaction between mentor and learner.[6]

Being familiar with the entire program prior to beginning the mentoring makes it easier to conduct mentoring; without familiarity, participants can be lost when there is no individual to take the lead. Good working relationships make the project easier and more fun for everyone involved. The individual taking the lead can be the mentor, whose input is vital in keeping others motivated in working through the project. Finally, familiarity with technology is a must for electronic mentoring.

As Peg Boyle Single and Richard M. Single point out, "E-mentoring is not a panacea; neither is it an inexpensive alternative to face-to-face mentoring."[7] E-mentoring is just another avenue in which to conduct mentoring. Early on, e-mentoring did not always meet the expectations of all involved. This is evident from the program that began in 1991 in Atlanta. For example, one of the participants "had no idea of how electronic mentoring was supposed to work or what I was supposed to do."[8] Another stated that

> *E-mentoring is not a panacea; neither is it an inexpensive alternative to face-to-face mentoring.*

"the messages I sent to the list were returned to me as undeliverable."[9] Still another expressed frustration on "gauging whether my messages are being understood. Silence in response to a posting may mean any number of things."[10] Retooling early e-mentoring programs helped to work out some of the problems. E-mentoring can level the playing field or can place everyone on equal footing. [11] Furthermore, these early programs provided professional and educational opportunities to underrepresented groups. Underrepresented groups, for example, may be professionals unable to attend conferences or those working as a solo librarian.

Case Study: E-mentoring a Protégé

Hilbun and Akin point out that "e-mentoring allows for partnering relationships to span departments or towns."[12] One opportunity that I had to e-mentor occurred while I was a member of the Research Committee, which is a component of the distance-learning section of Association of College and Research Libraries (ACRL). To promote research and scholarly publishing, the Research Committee decided to do e-mentoring in 2005. Members of the committee would be mentors for other librarians looking to conduct research. Committee members designed an e-mail that would be sent to an off-campus discussion list in January 2005. The e-mail stated:

Interested in mentoring a librarian in the research process? Right now, librarians have an opportunity to submit a proposal for the Off-Campus Library Services Conference in 2006, and the conference organizers are very interested in seeing more research-related proposals. If you would like [to] mentor a librarian, e-mail me at tunon@nova.edu and I will pair you with a research "mentee." For more information about the expectations for mentors and mentees, see the following:

> To promote research in the area of library services to distance learners, the Research Committee in the Distance Learning Section of ACRL is facilitating a research mentoring program to support upcoming professional librarians who are interested in conducting research in this area and reporting their research findings at the Off-Campus Library Services Conference in 2006. Experienced researchers who volunteer to participate as mentors will be paired with new professionals interested in conducting research.

Broadly, the mentoring guidelines will be as follows:

> Mentors will guide a mentee they are paired with in the areas of:
>
> - content
> - research methods
> - pointing mentee to experts who have conducted similar research
> - helping mentee on how to present and communicate ideas
> - providing feedback on research in progress
> - pointing mentee to relevant/key literature
>
> NOTE: Mentors are not intended to be editors of papers!

Mentees:

> - have a good idea of what they want to research
> - have a keen interest in the research topic
> - conduct a literature review[13]

Several librarians responded to the e-mail and were given the contact information of a member of the team desiring to mentor. I received an e-mail from a librarian working in distance learning at Brigham Young University. Mentoring a librarian from Brigham Young meant e-mentoring was the way to go because Utah is three-quarters of the way across the United States from southern Virginia. We were able to exchange documents via e-mail, whereas over the phone this would be impossible. In addition, the e-mentoring that the two of us undertook "broke down geographical and organizational barriers."[14]

> *The e-mentoring that the two of us undertook "broke down geographical and organizational barriers."*

The librarian at Brigham Young was considering writing a paper and giving a presentation at the 2006 Off-Campus Library Services Conference. The topic of the paper would be the career paths of distance-learning librarians. She stated in the first e-mail that she had never completed a formal research study before and desired help. In addition, she was thinking about conducting a survey.[15] As in other mentoring situations, I wanted it to be successful, and I felt that this mentoring relationship needed, as Hilbun and Akin state, "structure, objectives, administrative support, technical support, communication tools, training and support and finally assessment."[16] Because the two of us worked at universities, we had technical support and the communication tools available. We both had the training needed to conduct research and the administrative support inasmuch as academia requires faculty to present and publish. The objectives for the mentoring relationship were expressed in the original e-mail that was sent out on the list serve. The only item not covered in the e-mentoring relationship was assessment.

E-mail discussion between us led the protégé librarian to go with a survey that would be sent to the off-campus discussion list. I've found that answers to survey questions sometimes just about write your paper for you, and the findings can be easily reported at a conference. Ideas for the survey questions went back and forth between us for about two weeks. By mid-March, she had the survey ready and in a survey program. Prior to sending it to the discussion list, I took the survey for her to see how it flowed, and I looked for things that did not make sense. For the paper and presentation, we discussed that she should

> *This mentoring relationship needed, as Hilbun and Akin state, "structure, objectives, administrative support, technical support, communication tools, training and support and finally assessment."*

mention the population of subscribers of the discussion list and she needed to state how many were subscribed to the list at that time. On March 18, 2005, the survey was posted to the discussion list:

Fellow Off-Campers,

Please help me by completing a short survey I'm doing on the career paths of distance education librarians. The survey is anonymous and will take between 10 and 15 minutes to complete. I hope to present my findings at the upcoming Off-Campus Library Services Conference.

To access the survey, click on the link or copy and paste the link into your browser.

Thank you for your help.[17]

Writing a proposal for a conference presentation can be difficult. In this case, the survey had not been completed or analysis done. The protégé was unsure how to phrase the proposal. However, the proposal could state that a survey would be conducted regarding the background of librarians' decision to undertake distance librarianship. In addition, what qualifications did they determine to be most valuable? And what other responsibilities do the librarians have outside the distance part of the job? So the proposal could include what makes a distance librarian, what other jobs do they have, and what prepared the librarians for the job. The protégé wrote the proposal well, and her proposal got accepted for the program at the 2006 Off-Campus Library Services Conference.

By mid April, the mentee had 112 responses; this was lower than what she wanted for the presentation. At the time, there were 673 subscribers to the off-campus discussion list. The respondent's rate was just over 16 percent. However, that percentage can be representative of the entire number of surveys sent out. Concern over the numbers became less of a worry.

By August, the protégé had finished the first draft of the paper that would be published in the conference proceedings; she e-mailed me the draft and asked me to review it, which I did. My suggestions were placed in red within her article; I kept in mind to be gentle with comments and to be positive. When e-mailing the article back to her, I stated the comments were in red and were suggestions for clarity. Of course, I sent the message but no article. In the second e-mail, I sent the article along with this message:

Sorry! Here it is! Have you ever heard of the absentminded professor? Well, I am the absentminded librarian—too many things going on.[18]

The protégé then asked about the presentation as she was told not to just read the paper at the conference. She was instructed to go beyond what was in the paper during the presentation. She wanted to know if there were things that should be deleted. My answer was no, do not make deletions because readers would want to know as much as possible on the topic. However, personal experiences are great for presentations and can be intermingled through the data for a presentation. For instance, elaborating on challenges in serving distance students is always thought provoking. Figure 8.1, from her presentations slides, indicates that technology can be a challenge in distance learning. At Regent University, our distance students call or e-mail us with comments like, "I cannot get into the databases." My first questions are, "Are you doing it from work or home? If at work, is there a firewall?" My husband spent thirty years in the Coast Guard, and my first librarian position was as a cataloger at the Census Bureau; both military and government agencies usually have firewalls. I recommend that the student try accessing the databases from home.

One of my all-time favorite questions involved a non–Regent University patron calling the reference desk regarding usage of our databases. See figure 8.2 for what is shown on the database page. The first item aids distance students in troubleshooting when the librarians are not available for help; they then click on the second option. The third item is for Windows Vista users because of access problems to our databases by Vista users. The last option is for the five in-house public-access computers for visitors to the university. A non–Regent University patron did not understand why it did not work from her home computer. Stories like this make impressive anecdotes for presentations.

Figure 8.1

SKILLS AND CHALLENGES

Important Skills vs. Challenges

Qualifications	Challenges
Technology skills (75%)	Technology (17%)
Outreach skills (75%)	Communication (13%)
Public service skills (72%)	Lack of institutional awareness (13%)
Organizational skills (58%)	Equitable services (12%)

Source: From Allyson Washburn's 2006 presentation.

During the presentation, the protégé discussed the results of the study and then listed the questions for discussion in the session. (See figure 8.3.) She felt the discussion that ensued was probably the most constructive part of the presentation, not only for her, but for the attendees as well.

Once the protégé was finished with the PowerPoint presentation, she was just about ready for the conference.

The protégé and I both have attended various Off-Campus Library Services Conferences but had never met. The distance-learning section of ACRL holds meetings at both the Annual Conference and the Midwinter Meeting of the American Library Association. I became an active member of this section in

---

Figure 8.2

PART OF THE DATABASE WEB PAGE

PROBLEMS LOGGING IN?

First, click here to troubleshoot the problem.

Next, please try our ALTERNATE LOGIN PAGE using EZProxy.

Windows Vista users, please use this alternate/EZProxy page.

Public Area PC users—Please use this link to the database pages.

Source: Regent University Library Database Page, May 2009.

2004 and had not met the protégé. During the 2008 Annual Conference, the protégé and I finally met as a result of her joining the Research Committee, of which I was a member. She thanked me for my help reviewing her paper, advising her on the survey, and assisting in other ways.

Of those participating in the mentoring project done that year, the two of us as a team were the only ones to complete the mentoring process successfully. Other member mentors stated that contact between them and the protégés was only one or maybe two interactions. This left the mentors with feelings of frustration and of not having made a real difference with another individual. We are not sure how it affected the protégés because the person who matched them up did not follow through nor ask them how it went. In the future there should be more follow-up by the coordinator. Mentoring librarians might not know if they should take more initiative and e-mail the protégé to see how things are going. Often it could just be a matter of being overwhelmed by the job, and the mentor forgot to follow up.

> *Presenting and publishing are two pursuits that academic institutions expect librarians to achieve.*

There are many reasons why mentoring—especially electronic mentoring—fails. However, if the e-mentoring is successful, it can be fruitful and rewarding for both the mentor and protégé. The protégé I worked with gave a presentation at the Off-Campus Conference in 2006, and it was published in the conference proceedings. Presenting and publishing are two pursuits that academic institutions expect librarians to achieve. E-mentoring was a strong asset in my professional organization participation, it helped another librarian with advice regarding presenting and writing, and it afforded me the satisfaction of assisting another librarian.

Assessment can easily be completed upon the end of the mentoring relationship by sending an e-mail to the protégé regarding questions about the e-mentoring. Questions can be as simple as, Was the e-mentoring helpful to you? Would you take part in a mentoring relationship again? If the mentoring relationship was not helpful, why wasn't it? What could be improved?

Figure 8.3

PRESENTATION QUESTIONS

- Do distance education librarians perform essential functions that differ from other public service librarians?
- If so, why is there not more formal educaiton available in librar schools?
- Should we as a group be lobbying library schools to add curriculum related to distance education librarianship?
- If a career path were to be established, what would be the steps along that path?

Source: From Allyson Washburn's 2006 presentation.

NOTES

1. Janet Hilbun and Lynn Akin, "E-mentoring for Librarians and Libraries," *Texas Library Journal* 83, no. 1 (Spring 2007): 28.
2. Ibid.

3. Tami Echavarria, W. Bede Mitchell, Karen Liston Newsome, Thomas A. Peters, and Deleyne Wentz, "Encouraging Research through Electronic Mentoring: A Case Study," *College and Research Libraries* 56, no. 4 (July 1995): 353.

4. Ibid., 354.

5. Ibid., 355.

6. Bernard Nchindila, "Conditions for the Success of Mentoring: A Case Study," *Online Journal of Distance Learning Administration* 10, no. 11 (Summer 2007): 5.

7. Peg Boyle Single and Richard M. Single, "E-mentoring for Social Equity: Review of Research to Inform Program Development," *Mentoring and Tutoring* 13, no. 2 (August 2005): 301.

8. Echavarria, 356.

9. Ibid.

10. Ibid., 359.

11. Ibid., 354.

12. Hilbun and Akin, 28.

13. E-mail from Off-Campus Library Services List from January 23, 2005.

14. Ibid.

15. E-mail from Allyson Washburn from March 3, 2005.

16. Hilbun and Akin, 28.

17. E-mail from Off-Campus Library Services List from March 18, 2005.

18. E-mail correspondence from me to Allyson Washburn from August 3, 2005.

NINE

OTHER KINDS OF MENTORING IN THE LIBRARY FIELD

Mentoring, as discussed throughout this book, can take place in any type of library and may include a variety of situations:

- assisting students in completing internships;
- helping students complete course assignments;
- assisting individuals in deciding whether to pursue the library profession as a career choice;
- orienting and developing librarians within the library;
- mentoring librarians for tenure or promotion;
- working with and developing volunteers for the library; and
- assisting other librarians in writing for scholarly publications and giving presentations at conferences.

MENTORING STUDENTS

With online courses offered by many universities, mentoring can be as simple as a librarian proctoring exams. At Regent University Library, proctoring exams might involve helping students complete course work from other institutions. One student who needed to be proctored was a Regent student who was taking several courses at another institution because those Regent courses were not being offered within the next year. The student wanted to complete the course work in a certain time frame because of work restrictions. Another student had just married a U.S. Navy man; she was finishing up several classes from the University of Iowa. Her goal was to enter the graduate program in psychology and counseling at Regent University upon completion of her course work at the University of Iowa. When I proctor exams, I usually have the student come to the library during my time at the reference desk. I have the student take the exam at a reference table nearby in order to monitor them.

The reference librarians willingly accommodate students who need proctoring because we also have an active online program. Most of Regent University students do not need a proctor to complete an exam because the exams are administered online.

Regent University has a large number of distance learners who do not need proctored exams but do need assistance obtaining library materials. We give students the option to borrow any article or material in the library's circulating collection. For books not in the collection, we allow students the option to purchase them and be reimbursed for a local academic library card. Reimbursement can be up to one hundred dollars per year and for only one library card. We emphasize that the student should come to Regent University Library as the primary source for library assistance. The library also assists a large number of students not attending Regent University. As in most academic libraries, there are limits to some services (for example, interlibrary loan).

MENTORING LIBRARIANS

Discussion lists are another way librarians mentor each other. There are discussion lists that deal with technical services, reference, off-campus services, and many others. Librarians subscribe to discussion lists that best meet their needs. Discussion lists enable librarians to see what is taking place within other libraries and the problems they might be experiencing. Often they are utilized for tracking down answers to tough reference questions. Librarians use discussion lists to mentor each other and offer assistance. The following is a recent question posted to the COLLIB discussion list:

> Would anyone have a recommendation for where our library
> can dispose microfilm? Thanks for your help.[1]

One member recommended utilizing Safety Kleen, which is located in Baltimore, Maryland; the firm may be researched at www.Safety-Kleen.com.[2] Another discussion list member had a suggestion:

> If you have silver halide film (grey to black), it's likely that a local recycler will be willing to take it off your hands—in fact, they may pay you for the stuff. A little over a year ago, we shipped out some 2,600 pounds of silver halide microfilm; our local recycler gave us 90 cents/pound "as is"—i.e., still on reels and in the paperboard boxes. With the economy and commodity prices tanking, the price is likely lower nowadays. We also discarded some diazo film (blue), but couldn't find another option beyond putting it in our general dumpster.[3]

At times the answers can be positive along with a bit of sarcasm. Many of us have thought about our favorite filing place, the trash can or dumpster, when at the end of the road of options for recycling older materials. So asking a discussion list what others have done in a certain situation always provides other options. Often the requester will receive several dozen responses while others maybe none at all.

The following is a recent request from the reference discussion list.

> Can someone who works at a university with a robust language department or someone who writes Russian poetry/music help me with this reference question from one of our faculty members:
>
> > *"I need to know if they make a Russian rhyming dictionary. I have a friend who is a songwriter. She has a rhyming dictionary in English. Those are fairly common. She's having some songs translated into Russian and needs to know if they have a similar equivalent."*
>
> With very limited (read—almost no) success, I've looked for titles of Russian rhyming dictionaries in a few arts and humanities databases and in Book Index with Reviews. I'd like to be able to recommend a good title to him for his friend, but am at a loss at this point. Thank you for any tips/help/titles you can offer.[4]

This question could be viewed as a "toughie" especially because the patron needs a Russian rhyming dictionary. One respondent sent the following:

> I work at a small liberal arts college that teaches no Russian language classes, and I have zero familiarity with Slavic languages myself. (Talk about batting 1000!) But, I am a librarian, with all the powers endowed therein, so I'm gonna take a crack at this one.
>
> > Fedchenko, S. M. (1995). Slovar' russkikh sozvuchii : okolo 150,000 edinits. Moskva: Russkie slovari.
> >
> > Babakin, A. (1998). Slovar' rifm Iosifa Brodskogo. Tiumen' : Izd-vo IU. Mandriki.
> >
> > Babakin, A. (2000). Slovar' rifm Mariny TSvetaevoi. Tiumen' : Izd-vo IU. Mandriki.
>
> They all have the following subject heading: Russian language -- Rhyme -- Dictionaries.[5]

Another respondent indicated that she did not have a direct answer but provided the following:

> you might try asking the Slavic and Eastern European Library Reference Service at the University of Illinois–Urbana Champaign for assistance (www.library.illinois.edu/spx/). You can either chat with them or submit your question using their online form. I have used their service several times when trying to locate Russian materials for interlibrary loan and they always reply very quickly. They will even give suggestions as to which libraries carry the item you need. Hope that helps.[6]

A third respondent stated she contacted a friend regarding the question; the friend is a professor emeritus at a college in Pennsylvania. She sent the book title that he recommended while apologizing that some of the Russian characters were not coming through quite right.[7] Still another respondent sent the following information:

This looks like a possibility: Slovar' russkikh sozvuchii : okolo 150,000 edinits / Author: Fedchenko, S. M. Publication: Moskva : Russkie slovari, 1995 (a second ed. has date 2000).

There doesn't appear to be much availability but you could try interlibrary loan or a book dealer that specializes in Russian publications.[8]

Responses continued to flow in:

The one that I was able to find is available through Eastview .com based in Minneapolis, MN—a vendor specializing in books and periodicals from the countries once comprising the USSR. There is a rhyming dictionary which was published in 2003 (Title: Slovar'rifm: bolee 100,00 slovirifm = Rhyming dictionary: More than 100,000 words and rhymes) [may be found at www.eastview.com/russian/books/]. It is currently unavailable; however, if you contact eastview via e-mail (books@eastview.com), the staff can often locate the item for you through their office in Moscow.

Also, you may want to try contacting another vendor that I use, called MIPP, located in Minsk, Belarus. The contact person is Julia Maisak (e-mail: order@mippbooks .com). Although this title does not appear in MIPP's website (www.mippbooks.com), they can still track it down for you (they've located several titles for me in the past, and are very reliable).[9]

Another librarian searched WorldCat using the subject heading "Russian language rhyme dictionaries"; he stated that forty items were retrieved.[10] Response to the rhyming dictionary in Russian was outstanding; librarians are incredible in helping each other. Members of this discussion list are very helpful in answering inquiries because they might also end up with a tough question or would like to know what other libraries are doing to help make decisions.

Recently a faculty member desired to know why some electronic articles have the digital object identifier (DOI) while others do not. Discussion list respondents quickly let me know that the DOI is "voluntary and will vary by publisher, journal or organization."[11] One member pointed out that "the idea of a digital object identifier is one identifier [that] will bring up each unique article or document, while a URL may have session information and other one-time info."[12] Still another member pointed me to the DOI website and the following information:

> The Digital Object Identifier (DOI®) System is for identifying content objects in the digital environment. DOI® names are assigned to any entity for use on digital networks. They are used to provide current information, including where they (or information about them) can be found on the Internet. Information about a digital object may change over time, including where to find it, but its DOI name will not change.
>
> The DOI System provides a framework for persistent identification, managing intellectual content, managing metadata, linking customers with content suppliers, facilitating electronic commerce, and enabling automated management of media. DOI names can be used for any form of management of any data, whether commercial or noncommercial.[13]

This information allowed me to let the faculty member know what the DOI was and how it was used.

MENTORING SCHOOL LIBRARIANS

LM Net discussion list "is for practitioners helping practitioners, sharing new publications and upcoming conferences, asking for assistance or information, and linking schools through their library media centers."[14] This discussion list began in 1992 with a few dozen members; by 1995 there were more than 5,000 members. By October 2007 there were more than 12,000. School librarians are often the only media specialist at their school so having a virtual outlet for assistance is vital.[15] Members assist others in overcoming hurdles new media specialists face, for example, behavior of students, difficulties with teachers, and administration support. Often member librarians will offer to be a mentor for the new school librarian.[16] Erin Kilby states that it is a natural link between what children read and creative writing. She maintains that youth do not always see the relevance of yesterday's literature, like

School librarians are often the only media specialist at their school so having a virtual outlet for assistance is vital.

Little Women, by Louisa May Alcott, to their lives today. Furthermore, book discussions introduce young adults to the classic literature that most likely is taught in the classroom.[17]

Case Study: E-mentoring

Mentoring can take place between doctoral students and teaching faculty but also between doctoral students and librarians. Faculty can mentor by listening, advising, and being active role models for the doctoral student or new faculty member. Librarians can assist students in locating appropriate materials needed for course work or a dissertation. Often the doctoral student utilizes the librarian as someone who is a good listener to help him or her think through a problem.[18] Over the past three years, I have acted as a mentor for a doctoral student in the School of Communications and the Arts. This doctoral student liked discussing his assignment with someone; often his need was to think through the course work or assignments. More often than not I simply listened to what he was saying, following up with, Have you thought about . . . ? Librarians are quite adept in offering a listening ear and not imparting too much advice regarding the dissertation process except in locating resources. Librarians at Regent University Library do this type of mentoring with master's and doctoral students on a regular basis. Mentoring between the student and librarian works well for a number of reasons; the librarian does not sit in judgment of the student or project and is not impacting the acceptance or rejection of the topic. We are just here to listen and to be a guide to the appropriate resources.

Like Joanna Ptolomey, in her article on mentoring, I look for a wide variety of mentoring opportunities, but the ones selected are "based on [my] own personal situation and what [I am] looking for in a mentoring process."[19] Prior to attending the ALA's Annual Conference in Anaheim in 2008, I received an e-mail asking for volunteers in résumé reviewing for an hour while at the conference. The group asking for volunteers wanted librarians with experience in résumé reviewing. Here at Regent University Library, all of the librarians take part in interviewing new librarians and new library deans. I have been here for almost nine years and have reviewed applicant résumés and sat through five librarian interviews and one library dean interview. At the 2008 ALA Annual Conference I spent one hour early Sunday afternoon reviewing résumés and talking to the new librarians. I left the area for reviewing feeling highly motivated about the education and enthusiasm of the upcoming professionals. In 2009 I participated in résumé reviewing online.

D. Elizabeth Irish wrote about hiring and the interview process in 2005. Her article asked librarians what kind of "questions might be asked of librarians seeking new positions."[20] According to the article, there were four main requests:

- name what you look for when reviewing a résumé;
- name your favorite interview questions;
- name what impresses you most about a candidate; and
- name the best way to prepare for an interview.[21]

Relevant experience for the position applied for needs to be near the top of job experience because it is important. However, if it is an entry-level position, how much relevant experience can they have? Often applicants are asked for a cover letter; when I review the letter, I ask myself if it addresses the qualifications needed for the job. As I read, I also ask myself if the applicant has the potential to do well. When Regent University Library hired a new reference librarian in 2006, the applicant hired had been working as a systems librarian for a number of years with little time at the reference desk. However, looking further down his résumé, I noted that he had been evening supervisor in a circulation department while attending library school. This bit of information told me that he could easily do the job, and I was not disappointed; he was a great asset to the library and reference. When reviewing the résumé and interviewing for the position we were hiring for in 2007, I knew that the candidate had potential for reference in that she was enthusiastic in trying something new; this candidate had spent fifteen years in cataloging.

In her article, Irish identifies other significant questions for reviewing résumés:

- Does the candidate have job stability?
- Does the candidate have an error-free résumé?
- Does the candidate have excellent writing skills?
- Does the candidate have a growing level of responsibility?[22]

According to Irish, job jumping sends up a red flag to those doing the interviewing; moving jobs should be explained within a cover letter. Typos, spelling mistakes, and grammatical errors within the cover letter or résumé can also look bad for the applicant.[23]

Sundays at ALA conferences are generally reserved for committee meetings; the committee that I am on is no exception. So I attended the meeting in the morning and then reviewed résumés in the early afternoon. While reviewing résumés at the ALA Annual Conference in 2008, I kept the concepts discussed above in mind. I looked for grammatical errors, errors in formatting, and spelling. After asking applicants which type of library they were looking at, I made suggestions regarding the order of work experience listed on the résumé. For example, if the applicant was considering a public library, I suggested that the first several public library positions listed should be emphasized. If relevant experience was, for example, the fourth and fifth positions listed, then maybe they should be moved to the first and second positions, even if this experience came earlier in the applicant's career. I have often shuffled work experience on my résumé to address the requirements of the job. Résumé reviewing was very rewarding in that the individuals appreciated the assistance and that I helped someone else even in a small way.

> *Getting that first article accepted for publication can be intimidating for anybody, and I am no exception.*

MENTORING WRITING FOR PUBLICATION

One mentoring relationship that was exceptionally valuable for me began in 2003 and extended into 2004 and beyond when I began writing for publication. As a faculty member of an academic institution, I am expected to publish in peer-reviewed journals. Getting that first article accepted for publication can be intimidating for anybody, and I am no exception. I wrote on the development of library services to a new satellite campus. When I finished writing, I had the volunteer librarian proofread the article for me; I also had a tech-savvy graduate assistant help me with the appendixes. Upon completion, I sent the article electronically to Stephen H. Dew, editor of the *Journal of Library and Information Services in Distance Learning*, who responded back:

> Thank you for submitting your manuscript, "Red, White, and Blues" to the *Journal of Library and Information Services in Distance Learning*. I am glad to report that our reviewers believe that the manuscript has good potential, and it will be accepted for publication contingent upon you making a few changes. I have attached a copy of your manuscript and have made a few suggestions that are highlighted in yellow. Many of the recommendations are for minor things (commas, use of lowercase letters, etc.). Most of the changes will help with consistency, as well as aid readers in following your discussion.[24]

Dew shared with me some of the suggestions that the reviewers made regarding the article. Dew's suggestions about my article made me a better writer and pushed me to do more scholarly writing. I made the corrections to the article, and resubmitted it to Dew; the article appeared in volume one, issue three. A second article, cowritten with a colleague, was published a year later. This second article took less editing than the first because of Dew's wonderful editing assistance and mentoring on the first article. Dew began a mentoring relationship with me regarding publishing when I submitted the first article. His comments, advice, and being a teacher were invaluable to me. A piece of advice that I give others regarding writing is when something you've written is not accepted, do not take it personally. Just move on to the next topic of interest and try again, and perhaps you will encounter a writing mentor along the way.

Mentoring does not always require a long commitment; many of the mentoring opportunities in this chapter have been short term but very rewarding. Helping a patron by listening and locating materials can take half an hour or less; proctoring can be handled while other work is being completed; answering a question on a discussion list takes little time but is extremely helpful to the individual who needs the answer; reviewing résumés is easy and can help someone tremendously; and editing an article and helping it get published can change a life. Remember, there is never a mentoring project too small, which can be good for the librarian who is extremely busy.

Since I began mentoring others, I have been told by several librarians that they were on the verge of leaving the library profession until they began a mentoring relationship. Working with a mentor and changing jobs gave them a whole new perspective, and they remained in the library profession. Mentoring can nurture professionals both in the early stages of their careers and throughout their careers. With the graying of the profession, the younger generation needs our experience and knowledge to become tomorrow's leaders. Supporting others in their professional careers can be a rewarding activity to pursue. Have you ever had an individual simply say thank you for all your assistance? If not, when the opportunity arises to become involved in a mentoring relationship, take it.

NOTES

1. Discussion of the college libraries discussion list [collib-l-request@ala.org], accessed on June 12, 2009. Post by James McCloskey.
2. Discussion of the college libraries discussion list [collib-l-request@ala.org], accessed on June 12, 2009. Post by Nancy A. Cowherd.

3. Discussion of the college libraries discussion list [collib-l-request@ala.org], accessed on June 12, 2009. Post by Jim Parsons.

4. Discussion of library reference issues [LIBREF-L@LISTSERV.KENT.EDU], accessed on June 9, 2009. Post by Cathy Wilterding.

5. E-mail contact with Beth E. Fuchs, fuchsb@moravian.edu, received on June 18, 2009.

6. E-mail contact with Beth Kucera, bweixler@uwm.edu, received on June 18, 2009.

7. E-mail contact with Lisa Price, price12@umdnj.edu, received on June 18, 2009.

8. E-mail contact with Elaine M Coppola, emcoppol@syr.edu, received on June 18, 2009.

9. E-mail contact with James Kominowski, James_Kominowski@UManitoba.CA, received on June 18, 2009.

10. E-mail contact with Mark Schumacher, m_schuma@uncg.edu, received on June 18, 2009.

11. E-mail contact with Michael aka Dr Web, drweb@san.rr.com, received on September 29, 2009.

12. E-mail contact with Bryan M. Carson, bryan.carson@wku.edu, received on September 29, 2009.

13. International DOI Foundation, *The DOI System,* www.doi.org.

14. Blythe Bennett, "Librarian to Librarian: Mentoring on the LM_NRT," *Library Media Connection* 27, no. 5 (March/April 2009): 54.

15. Ibid.

16. Ibid., 55.

17. Erin Kilby, "School Librarian as Writing Mentor," *Knowledge Quest* 34, no. 4 (March/April 2006): 35–36.

18. Joseph C. Ugrin, Marcus D. Odom, and J. Michael Pearson, "Exploring the Importance of Mentoring for New Scholars: A Social Exchange Perspective," *Journal of Information Systems Education* 19, no. 3 (Fall 2008): 344.

19. Joanna Ptolomey, "Mentoring: Supporting the Library and Information Professional?" *Health Information and Libraries Journal* 25 (2008): 310.

20. D. Elizabeth Irish, "Winning the Hiring Game: What Candidates Can Learn from Interviewers," *Journal of Hospital Librarianship* 5, no. 1 (2005): 91.

21. Ibid., 92.

22. Ibid.

23. Ibid., 92–93.

24. E-mail correspondence with Stephen H. Dew, PhD, February 2, 2004.

APPENDIX A

REQUEST FOR INTERNSHIP FORM

Students requesting internships must fill out this form and get approval from their advisor and the faculty member coordinating the internship. The faculty coordinator must give a copy of the approved form to the SLIS office. The SLIS office staff will issue a permit and the student must then register by adding the class using the CRN#.

Name: _____ Campus Wide ID Number: _____

Student Address: _____

_____

Student Telephone Number Local: _____ Permanent:_____

Student e-mail address: _____

Semester and Year of Desired Internship: _____

Hours of Credit and Agency Contact Hours: (check one)

_____ 3 credits/150 hrs. for LS 570

_____ 3 credits/300 hrs. for LS 572 (School Media Only)

minimum 100 hrs./elementary and minimum 100 hrs./secondary

1. Please state your reason(s) for wanting to undertake this internship.
2. What specifically do you want to learn from this internship? You may cite the skills you would like to either gain or polish, the type of experiences or activities you would like to take part in, etc.

List courses completed in LS Program (including transfers):

_____
_____
_____
_____
_____

Student Signature/Date _____

Student's Faculty Advisor Signature/ Date _____

SLIS Faculty Internship Coordinator's Signature/Date _____

SLIS FACULTY Internship Coordinator fills in section below (not site supervisor)

_____

Name of Internship Agency: _____

Internship Agency Supervisor: _____

Internship Agency Address:_____ Phone:_____

E-mail:_____

APPENDIX B

REQUEST FOR ENROLLMENT IN PRACTICUM LSC 906

Name of Student: _____ Date: _____

Student ID#: _____

Mailing Address: _____

_____

Home Phone: _____ Work Phone: _____

E-mail: _____

Semester requesting enrollment   ❑ Fall   ❑ Spring   ❑ Summer   20__

Proposed Practicum Supervisor: _____

Mailing Address: _____

Work Phone: _____ E-mail: _____

What do you expect to achieve from this practicum?

_____

_____

_____

_____

Area of concentration in Library/Information Science:

_____

_____

_____

_____

Courses completed or in progress:

_____

_____

_____

_____

Anticipated date of graduation: _____

Faculty advisor:_____

Faculty advisor's signature and date:_____

DO NOT WRITE BELOW THIS LINE

Comments:

_____

_____

_____

APPENDIX C

SCHOOL OF INFORMATION STUDIES PROPOSAL FORM

This form is **required** to earn credit for an internship position. It *must* be submitted to the assignment box in *LMS – IST 971* (formerly WebCT) at least **one week prior** to the start of the work assignment.

Student Information

Name: _____ SU ID #: _____

Degree Program:　❑ B.S. (IM&T)　❑ IM　❑ TNM　❑ MSLIS

(School media students must use other form)

Distance Learning:　❑ Yes　❑ No

How many credit hours have you completed towards your degree? _____

Current Address: _____

City: _____ State: _____ Zip: _____ Phone _____

E-mail: _____

Gender:　❑ Female　❑ Male

Disability:　❑ Yes　❑ No

Ethnicity (Optional):　❑ African American　❑ American Indian/Alaskan Native

❑ Asian American/Pacific Islander　❑ Caucasian　❑ Hispanic　❑ Other _____

Are you a United States citizen?　❑ Yes　❑ No

If no, are you a permanent resident? _____

Semester your Internship will begin:　❑ Fall　❑ Spring　❑ Summer　Year:___

Semester in which you will register:　❑ Fall　❑ Spring　❑ Summer　Year:___

Number of credits: _____ (Remember, 50 work hours = 1 credit)

Is this your   ❑ 1st Internship through Information Studies?
                ❑ 2nd Internship through Information Studies?

Have you been involved in any type of experiential learning since you enrolled in college?   ❑ Yes   ❑ No

This is for a   ❑ paid internship   ❑ unpaid internship

Approximate dates of work block: From: _____ To: _____

Schedule (days, hours of work): _____

Academic Advisor: _____ Faculty Supervisor:_____

Internship Site Information

Organization Name: _____

Address: _____

City: _____ State: _____ Zip: _____

Phone: _____ Fax _____

E-mail: _____ URL: _____

Site Supervisor

Name: (Mr. or Ms.) _____

Title: _____ E-mail: _____

Phone: _____ Fax:_____

Additional Contact (if any): _____

Title: _____ E-mail: _____

Phone: _____ Fax: _____

PLEASE PROVIDE A BRIEF DESCRIPTION OF YOUR PROPOSED PROJECTS/ ACTIVITIES. (This is only your proposed activities. We realize this may change once you are involved in the internship.)

_____

_____

_____

_____

_____

APPENDIX D

VIDEO VIEWING INFORMATION: AFR MANUAL FORM

Labels on Case: _____

Labels on Cassette:_____

Format (cassette length): ¾" U-matic ____ VHS _____ Beta _____ 1" _____ Other_____

Loose print information with tape?   Yes: _____   No: _____

Information from Viewing

Color and sound test screen?   Yes: _____   No: _____

Running Times:_____Production Screen Information:_____

Before AFR Event: _____Title:_____

Of AFR Event: _____Producer:_____

After AFR Event: _____Length: _____

Total Running Time: _____Date: _____

Location: _____

Credits: Yes: ____ No: ____ See back if Yes.

Event / Topic / Speaker(s) Related to AFR: _____
_____
_____

Events / Topics / Speakers Not Related to AFR: _____
_____
_____

Notes, other considerations: _____
_____
_____

Video Quality: 1   2   3   4   5   Notes: _____

Audio Quality: 1   2   3   4   5   Notes: _____

Viewed by: _____ Date: _____ Location: _____

Playback Machine: _____

[For manual recording of information from videos.] [DG 6/5/07] [RUL Spec. Coll. & Arch.]

APPENDIX E

PROMOTION REVIEW TIMETABLE

Tenure or Promotion Review Timetable and Process

In the case of an ordinary tenure or promotion review, the general timetable is as follows:

1. By the beginning of the semester preceding the academic year in which the faculty member is to be reviewed for tenure or promotion, the dean will give the faculty member guidelines for compiling her/his section of the dossier and a complete timetable for the review process.

2. By November 1, the tenure candidate submits her/his dossier to the dean.

3. The tenured faculty of the school shall select a tenure review committee. The committee:
   a. Examines the candidate's dossier.
   b. Meets to discuss the candidate's qualifications and contributions in relation to the mission of the school.
   c. Determines whether the candidate demonstrates the level of distinction and potential expected by the university.
   d. May solicit additional evaluations from individuals outside the university who are acknowledged authorities in the field relevant to the candidate's academic specialty.
   e. By December 15, makes a recommendation to the dean on whether or not to award tenure or promotion. The recommendation contains the substance of their discussions and the reasons for the recommendation.

4. In the case of tenure (not promotion), the dean reviews the recommendation based on the candidate's merit and the long-term needs of the school. This includes:
   a. The long-term enrollment.
   b. The need for an additional specialist in the faculty member's area of specialization, particularly in light of the school's mission.
   c. The tenure structure of the school. (Although no maximum percentage of faculty is established, the dean must take into account the need for

flexibility in course offerings and the desirability of a tenure structure that will allow openings for new tenured faculty in the ensuing decades so that new areas of specialization and new needs can be met.)

5. By February 1, the dean makes a recommendation to the vice president for academic affairs regarding the award of tenure or promotion, including a summary report of her/his deliberations and the reasons for the recommendations, as well as the recommendation of the Tenure Review Committee.

6. By February 15, the vice president for academic affairs reviews the recommendations of the dean and the Tenure Review Committee and makes a recommendation to the president regarding the award of tenure or promotion.

7. By March 1, the president notifies the candidate of her/his recommendation. If the recommendation is positive, it is forwarded to the Board of Trustees. If the recommendation is negative, the reasons must be stated in a written letter to the candidate. The candidate may request a meeting with the president to review her/his decision to not recommend tenure.

8. Generally by April 30, the Board of Trustees makes a decision on the matter at their spring meeting. Their decision is final.

The candidate may withdraw her/his tenure or promotion application at any stage of the process.

BIBLIOGRAPHY

ACRL Committee on the Status of Academic Librarians. "A Guideline for the Appointment, Promotion, and Tenure of Academic Librarians." *College and Research Libraries News* 66, no. 9 (June 2005): 668–676.

Ali, A. Nazim, Harold C. Young, and Nasser M. Ali. "Determining the Quality of Publications and Research for Tenure or Promotion Decisions: A Preliminary Checklist to Assist." *Library Review* 45, no. 1 (1996): 39–53.

Arnold, Bruce. "Information Commons: Cooperation Makes It Work." *PNLA Quarterly* 73, no. 1 (Fall 2008): 37–38.

Badke, William. "Professors and Personal Information Literacy." *Online* 33, no. 1 (January/February 2009): 47–49.

Barnes, Newkirk. "Doing It All: First Year Challenges for New Academic Reference Librarians." *The Reference Librarian* 47, no. 1 (2007): 51–61.

Bateman, Mark, and Richard Leonard. "Social Club or Compulsory Experience: Reflections on the Proper Role of Volunteers in Records Offices." *Journal of Society of Archives* 20, no. 1 (1999): 75–84.

Bates, Mary Ellen. "The Newly Minted MLS: What Do We Need to Know Today?" *Searcher* 6, no. 5 (May 1998): 30–33.

Belic, K., and D. Surla. "User Friendly Web Application, for Bibliographic Material Processing." *Electronic Library* 26, no. 3 (2008): 400–410.

Benefiel, Candace R., Jeannie P. Miller, Pixey Anne Mosley, and Wendie Arant-Kaspar. "Service to the Profession: Definitions, Scope, and Value." *Reference Librarian* 73 (2001): 361–372.

Bennett, Blythe. "Librarian to Librarian: Mentoring on the LM_NRT." *Library Media Connection* 27, no. 5 (March/April 2009): 54–56.

Bicksler, Sandra. "New Colleagues: A Program for Mentoring School Library Media Specialists." *Knowledge Quest* 33, no. 1 (September/October 2004): 28.

Bissett, Cindy. "TAFE Tasmania Living Writers' Week—Marketing Your Library by Holding Innovative Events." *Incite* 30, no. 3 (March 2009): 24–25.

Blue, Ana Rosa. "Transforming Library Service through Information Commons: Case Studies for the Digital Age. *Feliciter* 55, no. 1 (2009): 27.

Bradigan, Pamela S., and Carol A. Mularski. "Evaluation of Academic Librarians' Publications for Tenure and Initial Promotion." *Journal of Academic Librarianship* (September 1996): 360–65.

Brown, Stephanie Willen. "The Reference Interview: Theories and Practice." *Library Philosophy and Practice* 10, no. 1 (Spring 2008): 1–8.

Buchanan, William E. "Volunteerism in Small and Rural Public Libraries in Pennsylvania." *Bookmobile and Outreach Services* 11, no. 2 (2008): n.p.

Cirasella, Jill. "You and Me and Google Makes Three: Welcoming Google into the Reference Interview." *Library Philosophy and Practice* 9, no. 3 (Summer 2007): 1–8.

Crump, Michele, Carol Drum, and Colleen Seale. "Establishing a Pre-tenure Review Program in an Academic Library." *Library Administration and Management* 22, no. 1 (Winter 2008): 31–36.

Dagg, Emily. "Middle School Volunteers with Special Needs at the Denver Public Library." *Young Adult Library Services* (Summer 2006): 40.

De Pree, Max, and Walter C. Wright Jr. *Mentoring: Two Voices.* Pasadena: De Pree Leadership Center, 2003.

Druschel, J. "Cost Analysis of an Automated and Manual Cataloging and Book Processing Process." *Journal of Library Automation* 14, no. 1 (March 1981): 24–49.

Duff, C. S. *Learning from Other Women How to Benefit from the Knowledge, Wisdom, and Experience of Female Mentors.* www.netLibrary.com/urlapi .asp?action=summary&v=1&bookid=43909. Note: an electronic book accessible through the World Wide Web.

Echavarria, Tami, W. Bede Mitchell, Karen Liston Newsome, Thomas A. Peters, and Deleyne Wentz. "Encouraging Research through Electronic Mentoring: A Case Study." *College and Research Libraries* 56, no. 4 (July 1995): 352–361.

Enger, Brock. "Using Citation Analysis to Develop Core Book Collections in Academic Libraries." *Library and Information Science Research* 31, no. 2 (April 2009): 107–12.

Evans, Darrell A. "Learning to Be a Leader/Mentor." *Mentoring and Tutoring* 15, no. 4 (November 2007): 385–90.

Faculty and Academic Policy Handbook. Regent University. www.regent.edu/ academics/academic_affairs/faculty_handbook.cfm#library_faculty.

Fennewald, Joseph, and John Stachacz. "Recruiting Students to Careers in Academic Libraries." *College and Research Libraries News* 66, no. 2 (2005): 120–22.

Field, Judith. "Mentoring: A Natural Act for Information Professionals?" *New Library World* 102, no. 1166/1167 (2001): 269–73.

Flaherty, J. *Coaching: Evoking Excellence in Others.* www.netLibrary.com/urlapi .asp?action=summary&v=1&bookid=34013. Note: an electronic book accessible through the World Wide Web.

Floyd, Deborah M., Gloria Colvin, and Yasar Bodurr. "A Faculty-Librarian Collaboration for Developing Information Literacy Skills among Preservice Teachers." *Teaching and Teacher Education* 24, no. 2 (February 2008): 368–76.

Fulton, Tara Lynn. "Mentor Meets Telemachus: The Role of the Department Head in Orienting and Inducting the Beginning Reference Librarian." *The Reference Librarian* 22, no. 26 (1990): 257–73.

Ghouse, Nikhat, and Jennifer Church-Duran. "And Mentoring for All: The KU Libraries' Experience." *Portal: Libraries and the Academy* 8, no. 4 (2008): 373–86.

Giers, Ralph, and Lillie J. Seward. "I Hear You Say . . . Peer Coaching for More Effective Reference Service." *The Reference Librarian* 9, no. 22 (November 1988): 245–60.

Goulding, Anne. "Engaging with Community Engagement: Public Libraries and Citizen Involvement." *New Library World* 110, no. 1/2 (2009): 37–51.

Harwood, Dorren, and Charlene McCormack. "Growing Our Own: Mentoring Undergraduate Students." *Journal of Business and Finance Librarianship* 13, no. 3 (2008): 201–15.

Hass, V. Heidi, and Tony White. "Mentorship Task Force Report, Professional Development Committee, ARLIS/NA." *Art Documentation* 24, no. 2 (2005): 49–56.

Hilbun, Janet, and Lynn Akin. "E-mentoring for Librarians and Libraries." *Texas Library Journal* 83, no. 1 (Spring 2007): 28–32.

Hildebrand, M., and E. Rudd. "Processing of Government Publications in the State Library of New South Wales." *Cataloging and Classification Quarterly* 18, no. 3/4 (1994): 155–65.

Irish, D. Elizabeth. "Winning the Hiring Game: What Candidates Can Learn from Interviewers." *Journal of Hospital Librarianship* 5, no. 1 (2005): 91–96.

Jones, Sherri, and Jessica Kayongo. "Identifying Student and Faculty Needs through LibQUAL: An Analysis of Qualitative Survey Comments." *College and Research Libraries* 69, no. 6 (November 2008): 493–509.

Kanyengo, Christine W. "Meeting Collection Development Needs in Resource Poor Settings: The University of Zambia Medical Library Experience." *Collection Building* 28, no. 1 (2009): 26–30.

Kaplan, Allison. "Is Your School Librarian 'Highly Qualified'?" *Phi Delta Kappan* (December 2007): 300–303.

Kaplowitz, Joan. "Mentoring Library School Students—a Survey of Participants in the UCLA/GSLIS Mentor Program." *Special Libraries* 83, no. 4 (Fall 1992): 219–33. www.sla.org/speciallibraries/ISSN00386723V83N4.PDF.

Kenney, Barbara Ferrer. "Revitalizing the One-Shot Instruction Session Using Problem-Based Learning." *Reference and User Services Quarterly* 47, no. 4 (2008): 386–91.

Kilby, Erin. "School Librarian as Writing Mentor." *Knowledge Quest* 34, no. 4 (March/April 2006): 35–36.

Knecht, Mike, and Kevin Reid. "Modularizing Information Literacy Training via the Blackboard E-community." *Journal of Library Administration* 49, no. 1 (2009): 1–9.

Kreitz, P. A., and J. DeVries. *Recruiting, Training, and Retention of Science and Technology Librarians.* Binghamton, NY: Haworth Information Press, 2006.

Kuyper-Rushing, Lois. "A Formal Mentoring Program in a University Library: Components of a Successful Experiment." *Journal of Academic Librarianship* 27, no. 6 (November 2001): 440–45.

Lagesten, Carin E. "Students as Library Leaders: Student Team Builds Leadership Skills While Helping to Battle Budget Cuts." *Teacher Librarian* 34, no. 5 (June 2007): 45–47.

Law, Margaret. "Mentoring Programs: In Search of the Perfect Model." *Feliciter* 3 (2001): 146–48.

Lawson, Karen G., and Nancy L. Pelzer. "Assessing Technology-Based Projects for Promotion and/or Tenure in ARL Academic Libraries." *College and Research Libraries* 60, no. 5 (September 1999): 464–76.

Lee, Marta. "Growing Librarians: Mentorship in an Academic Library." *Library Leadership and Management* 23, no. 1 (Winter 2009): 31–37.

Lee, Marta, and Sandy Yaegle. "Information Literacy at an Academic Library: Development of a Library Course in an Online Environment." *Journal of Library and Information Services in Distance Learning* 2, no. 3 (2006): 33–44.

Lewkus-Faller, M. "Managing the Student Budget." *Community and Junior College Libraries* 2, no. 3 (Spring 1984): 61–72.

Lillare, Linda L., Scott Norwood, Kate Wise, Jan Brooks, and Royce Kitts. "Embedded Librarians: MLS Students as Apprentice Librarians in Online Courses." *Journal of Library Administration* 49 (2009): 11–22.

Little, J. W., L. Nelson, and ERIC Clearinghouse on Educational Management. *A Leader's Guide to Mentor Training.* Eugene, OR: ERIC Clearinghouse on Educational Management, 1990.

Lubans Jr., John. "Coaching for Results." *Library Administration and Management* 20, no. 2 (Spring 2006): 86–89.

Martorana, Janet, Eunice Schoeder, Lucia Snowhill, and Andrea L. Duda. "A Focus on Mentorship in Career Development." *Library Administration and Management* 18, no. 4 (Fall 2003): 198–202.

McKenzie, Betsy. "Why do Librarians Eat Their Young? And How Law Librarians Can Make Things Better." *The One-Person Library* 25, no. 5 (September 2008): 7–9.

Mellon, Constance A., and Diane D. Kester. "Online Library Education Programs: Implications for Rural Students." *Journal of Education for Library and Information Science* 45, no. 3 (Summer 2004): 210–20.

Meloni, Christine. "Mentoring the Next Generation of Library Media Specialists." *Library Media Connection* (January 2008): 32–33.

Metz, Ruth. *Coaching in the Library.* Chicago: American Librarian Association, 2001.

Miller, W., and R. M. Pellen. *Current Practices in Public Libraries.* Binghamton, NY: Haworth Information Press, 2006.

Moore, Alanna Aiko, Michael J. Miller, Veronda J. Pitchford, and Ling Hwey Jeng. "Mentoring in the Millennium: New Views, Climate and Actions." *New Library World* 109, no. 1/2 (2008): 75–86.

Munde, Gail. "Beyond Mentoring: Toward the Rejuvenation of Academic Libraries." *Journal of Academic Librarianship* 26, no. 3 (May 2000): 171–75.

Nchindila, Bernard. "Conditions for the Success of Mentoring: A Case Study." *Online Journal of Distance Learning Administration* 10, no. 11 (Summer 2007): 1–14.

Nicol, Erica, and Corey M. Johnson. "Volunteers in the Library: Program Structure, Evaluation and Theoretical Analysis." *Reference and Users Services Quarterly* 48, no. 2 (2008): 154–63.

Nixon, Judith M. "Growing Your Own Leaders: Succession Planning in Libraries." *Journal of Business and Finance Librarianship* 13, no. 3 (2008): 249–60.

Olivas, Antonia. "Mentoring New Librarians: The Good, the Bad and the Ugly." In *Staff Development Strategies That Work!* edited by Georgie L. Donovan and Miguel A. Figueroa, 62. New York: Neal-Schuman, 2009.

Osif, Bonnie. "Successful Mentoring Programs: Examples from Within and Without the Academy." *Journal of Business and Finance Librarianship* 13, no. 3 (2008): 335–47.

The Oxford English Dictionary. 2nd ed. J. A. Simpson, ed. Oxford: Oxford University Press, 1991.

Pennsylvania State University. "Guideline UL-HRG07 Promotion and Tenure Criteria Guidelines." Pennsylvania State University. www.libraries.psu .edu/psul/jobs/facultyjobs/p_t_guidelines.html.

Price, Apryl C. "How to Make a Dollar out of Fifteen Cents: Tips for Electronic Collection Development." *Collection Building* 28, no. 1 (2009): 31–34.

Ptolomey, Joana. "Mentoring: Supporting the Library and Information Professional?" *Health Information and Libraries Journal* 25 (2008): 309–12.

Ralli, Tony. "Professionalism—Does It Count?" *Australian Academic Research Libraries* 21, no. 1 (September 1990): 171–77.

Reynolds, Latisha. "Diversity Dispatch: Take a Deep Breath and Call Your Mentor." *Kentucky Libraries* 72, no. 3 (Summer 2008): 23–24.

Rhoades, James G., and Arianne Hartsell. "Marketing First Impressions: Academic Libraries Creating Partnerships and Connections at New Student Orientations." *Library Philosophy and Practice* (August 2008): 1–11.

Richey, Debora. "Inside Internships: A Reference Librarian's Perspective." *College and Research Libraries* 40, no. 1 (1997): 107–15.

Ries-Taggart, Jennifer T. "Brighton Memorial Offers Reading Partnership with Seniors." *Public Libraries* 48, no. 1 (January/February 2009): 11–12.

Riley, Cheryl, and Barbara Wales. "Academic Librarians and Mentoring Teams: Building Tomorrow's Doctorates." *Technical Services Quarterly* 14, no. 3 (1997): 1–10.

Rothman, Miriam. "Lessons Learned: Advice to Employers from Interns." *Journal of Education for Business* (January/February 2007): 140–44.

Selby, Courtney. "The Evolution of the Reference Interview." *Legal Reference Services Quarterly* 26, no. 1 (2007): 35–46.

Sevetson, Andrea. "Editor's Corner: Thanking Our Mentors." *DttP: Document to the People* 35, no. 1 (Spring 2007): 4.

Shelton, Kay. "Starting a Volunteer Program in a Community College Library." *Community and Junior College Libraries* 14, no. 3 (2008): 161–77.

Shonrock, Diana D. "NextGen Librarians: Interviews with RUSA Interns." *Reference and User Services Quarterly* 46, no. 2 (Winter 2006): 7–11.

Single, Peg Boyle, and Richard M. Single. "E-mentoring for Social Equity: Review of Research to Inform Program Development." *Mentoring and Tutoring* 13, no. 2 (August 2005): 301–20.

Spires, Todd. "The Busy Librarian: Prioritizing Tenure and Dealing with Stress for Academic Library Professionals." *Illinois Libraries* 84, no. 4 (Spring 2007): 101–8.

Stone, F. M. *Coaching, Counseling and Mentoring: How to Choose and Use the Right Technique to Boost Employee Performance.* www.netlibrary.com/urlapi .asp?action=summary&v=1&bookid=437. Note: an electronic book accessible through the World Wide Web.

Sweeny, Barry. "Is Informal or Formal Mentoring Needed?" International Mentoring Association web page. (2001). www.mentoring-association .org/Formalinformal.html.

Trotta, M. *Supervising Staff: A How-to-Do-It Manual for Librarians.* New York: Neal-Schuman, 2006.

Ugrin, Joseph C., Marcus D. Odom, and J. Michael Pearson. "Exploring the Importance of Mentoring for New Scholars: A Social Exchange Perspective." *Journal of Information Systems Education* 19, no. 3 (Fall 2008): 343–50.

Wagner, Tory. "Look, It's Books! Marketing Your Library with Displays and Promotions." *Catholic Library World* 79, no. 3 (March 2009): 229.

Wandersee, Janene R. "Library Checkup: Medical Residents and Fellows' Library Questionnaire Response." *Journal of Hospital Librarianship* 8, no. 3 (2008): 323–31.

Warren, Patricia. "Inside Internship: A Student's Perspective." *College and Undergraduate Libraries* 4, no. 1 (1997): 117–23.

Weingart, Sandra J., Carol A. Kochan, and Anne Hedrich. "Safeguarding Your Investment: Effective Orientation for New Employees." *Library Administration and Management* 12, no. 3 (Summer 1998): 156–58. http://0-vnweb.hwwilsonweb.com.library.regent.edu/hww/results/ results_single_fulltext.jhtml;hwwilsonid=PQ5FDYSNVBBKLQA3DILCFGG ADUNGIIV0.

Wittkopf, B. J., Association of Research Libraries, Office of Leadership and Management Services, Association of Research Libraries, and Systems and Procedures Exchange Center. *Mentoring Programs in ARL Libraries: A SPEC Kit.* Washington, D.C.: Association of Research Libraries, Office of Leadership and Management Services, 1999.

Wright Jr., Walter C. *The Gift of Mentors.* Pasadena, CA: De Pree Leadership Center, 2001.

Zhang, Sha Li, Susan J. Matveyeva, and Nancy Deyoe. "From Scratch: Developing an Effective Mentoring Program." *Chinese Librarianship: An International Electronic Journal* 24. www.iclc.us/cliej/cl24ZDM.html.

INDEX

In this index, LS means library school.

You may also be interested in

BE A GREAT BOSS: ONE YEAR TO SUCCESS
Catherine Hakala-Ausperk

To help library managers improve their skills and acumen, renowned speaker and trainer Catherine Hakala-Ausperk presents a handy self-study guide to the dynamic role of being a boss. This workbook is organized in 52 modules, designed to cover a year of weekly sessions but easily adaptable for any pace.

ISBN: 978-0-8389-1068-9 / 232 PGS / 8.5" × 11"

ORGANIZATIONAL STORYTELLING FOR LIBRARIANS: USING STORIES FOR EFFECTIVE LEADERSHIP
Kate Marek

Just as literature can be used for learning, the power of storytelling can be very effective when applied to leadership. Applying solid management principles to a library setting, Kate Marek provides the tools and explains the process of leading and

ISBN: 978-0-8389-1079-5 / 136 PGS / 6" × 9"

COACHING IN THE LIBRARY: A MANAGEMENT STRATEGY FOR ACHIEVING EXCELLENCE, SECOND EDITION
Ruth F. Metz

Experienced librarian and coach Ruth Metz outlines a focused and results-oriented plan for achieving the best results from staff members through a coaching style of management.

ISBN: 978-0-8389-1037-5 / 112 PGS / 8.5" × 11"

SUCCESSION PLANNING IN THE LIBRARY: DEVELOPING LEADERS, MANAGING CHANGE
Paula M. Singer with Gail Griffith

Drawing on her expertise as a leading consultant on human resources issues in the library, Paula Singer addresses the often fraught issue of planning for change at all levels of an organization.

ISBN: 978-0-8389-1036-8 / 160 PGS / 8.5" × 11"

Order today at www.alastore.ala.org or 866-746-7252!

ALA Store purchases fund advocacy, awareness, and accreditation programs for library professionals worldwide.

DEC 0 5 2011

CPSIA information can be obtained at www.ICGtesting.com
Printed in the USA
LVOW032034121011

250233LV00006B/41/P

9 780838 935934